SYRIA AFTER THE MISSILE STRIKES: POLICY OPTIONS

HEARING

BEFORE THE

COMMITTEE ON FOREIGN AFFAIRS
HOUSE OF REPRESENTATIVES

ONE HUNDRED FIFTEENTH CONGRESS

FIRST SESSION

APRIL 27, 2017

Serial No. 115–27

Printed for the use of the Committee on Foreign Affairs

Available via the World Wide Web: http://www.foreignaffairs.house.gov/ or
http://www.gpo.gov/fdsys/

U.S. GOVERNMENT PUBLISHING OFFICE

25–261PDF   WASHINGTON : 2017

For sale by the Superintendent of Documents, U.S. Government Publishing Office
Internet: bookstore.gpo.gov   Phone: toll free (866) 512–1800; DC area (202) 512–1800
Fax: (202) 512–2104   Mail: Stop IDCC, Washington, DC 20402–0001

COMMITTEE ON FOREIGN AFFAIRS

EDWARD R. ROYCE, California, *Chairman*

CHRISTOPHER H. SMITH, New Jersey
ILEANA ROS-LEHTINEN, Florida
DANA ROHRABACHER, California
STEVE CHABOT, Ohio
JOE WILSON, South Carolina
MICHAEL T. McCAUL, Texas
TED POE, Texas
DARRELL E. ISSA, California
TOM MARINO, Pennsylvania
JEFF DUNCAN, South Carolina
MO BROOKS, Alabama
PAUL COOK, California
SCOTT PERRY, Pennsylvania
RON DeSANTIS, Florida
MARK MEADOWS, North Carolina
TED S. YOHO, Florida
ADAM KINZINGER, Illinois
LEE M. ZELDIN, New York
DANIEL M. DONOVAN, JR., New York
F. JAMES SENSENBRENNER, JR.,
  Wisconsin
ANN WAGNER, Missouri
BRIAN J. MAST, Florida
FRANCIS ROONEY, Florida
BRIAN K. FITZPATRICK, Pennsylvania
THOMAS A. GARRETT, JR., Virginia

ELIOT L. ENGEL, New York
BRAD SHERMAN, California
GREGORY W. MEEKS, New York
ALBIO SIRES, New Jersey
GERALD E. CONNOLLY, Virginia
THEODORE E. DEUTCH, Florida
KAREN BASS, California
WILLIAM R. KEATING, Massachusetts
DAVID N. CICILLINE, Rhode Island
AMI BERA, California
LOIS FRANKEL, Florida
TULSI GABBARD, Hawaii
JOAQUIN CASTRO, Texas
ROBIN L. KELLY, Illinois
BRENDAN F. BOYLE, Pennsylvania
DINA TITUS, Nevada
NORMA J. TORRES, California
BRADLEY SCOTT SCHNEIDER, Illinois
THOMAS R. SUOZZI, New York
ADRIANO ESPAILLAT, New York
TED LIEU, California

AMY PORTER, *Chief of Staff*   THOMAS SHEEHY, *Staff Director*
JASON STEINBAUM, *Democratic Staff Director*

(II)

CONTENTS

SYRIA AFTER THE MISSILE STRIKES: POLICY OPTIONS

THURSDAY, APRIL 27, 2017

House of Representatives,
Committee on Foreign Affairs,
Washington, DC.

The committee met, pursuant to notice, at 10:07 a.m., in room 2172 Rayburn House Office Building, Hon. Edward Royce (chairman of the committee) presiding.

Chairman ROYCE. This hearing will come to order.

The title of this hearing, colleagues, is Syria After the Missile Strikes: Policy Options.

Some of us had the opportunity over the last week with what are called the White Helmets and these are Syrian volunteers. These are civil society people. I think one who I talked to was an accountant. She was an accountant. Another one was a firefighter. But they come from all ethnic, and religious, and political factions inside Syria. What these civil society people all have in common is that they are the ones that you see on television who are rushing in to collapsing buildings to rescue people, a stranger or a friend, and then try to take them to the hospital and many of these hospitals are under bombardment. They have saved some 70,000 people. And if you have an opportunity, you should hear their stories and hear their plea that we all try to use whatever political leverage we have to try to get Assad and the other factions to the table. But this morning we consider options for Syria in the wake of this month's renewed chemical attacks by Bashar al-Assad and the bold response we saw from the administration.

On April 4th, facing an opposition offensive against key infrastructure, the regime in Syria launched a sarin gas attack in southern Idlib Province. Eighty-five people—including many children—died from that attack. The effects of sarin gas are immediate: The nose runs, eyes water, the mouth drools and this progresses to convulsions, paralysis, and in many cases death in less than 10 minutes. There is a reason indiscriminate killing of chemicals and chemical attacks cross a "red line." There is a reason for that. And the reason is it is abhorrent.

Assad was sending a demoralizing message to the civilian population there. It was: "I can kill with impunity—with some of the worst weapons of war—and no one will help you."

But in a matter of days, the Syrian regime did pay a price. Two days later, nearly 60 Tomahawk missiles—fired from U.S. Navy ships operating in international waters—targeted the Syrian airfield from which the sarin attacks had launched. In a limited and targeted response, U.S. forces destroyed 23 Syrian warplanes and supporting infrastructure.

This use of force was proportional, legitimate, and welcomed by our allies in the region and around the world. For after 6 years of unrestrained murder of Syrians, Assad was finally on the receiving end. Finally, "red lines" mattered. Finally, the United States was leading. And this week, the Treasury Department sanctioned 270 individuals involved in Syria's production of chemical weapons.

Now, having taken military action, the United States has a chance to take Syria policy on a different path. As one witness will testify today, "Determined U.S. leadership backed up by the credible and now proven threat of force presents the best opportunity in years to strong-arm actors on the ground into a phase of meaningful de-escalation, out of which eventually a durable negotiation process may result."

A good place to start this forceful diplomacy would be to make Russia and Iran pay a price for supporting Assad. So far, they have had no incentive to negotiate an end to the conflict in Syria, as they have been able to pursue their goals with little cost. That calculus would surely change if Mr. Engel's Caesar Syria Civilian Protection Act was passed by the Congress, signed into law, and vigorously enforced. This sweeping sanctions bill is guaranteed to get attention in Moscow and Tehran, and give the U.N.-backed process aimed at finding a political solution a chance.

And while the administration sticks to an "ISIS first" strategy, this, too, can push the political process along. As U.S.-backed forces gain ground in the east, Assad could be confined to the west, opening up sanctuaries in which Syrians might find refuge and establish basic governance. From there, the United States and their allies must work together to advance a plausible vision of a post-Assad Syria.

This won't be easy but Syria cannot keep going on and on like this. That is not in our humanitarian interest, not in the interest of the region, or America's national security interest. This has to change.

I know turn to the ranking member, who has long been focused on this conflict, for his opening statement.

Mr. ENGEL. Thank you very much, Mr. Chairman. And let me also thank our witnesses and welcome you all to the Foreign Affairs Committee.

This morning, the committee will continue its examination of a challenge that for more than 6 years global powers have been unable or unwilling to resolve: The brutal war that Bashar al-Assad and his enablers have waged against the people of Syria. Hundreds of thousands are dead at the hands of this butcher. Millions more have been driven from their homes and every time the potential for a resolution has been in sight, Assad has been granted another lifeline.

The missile strike earlier this month escalated American involvement against Assad to a new level. I think the response was appropriate. But a few weeks down the road, we are left asking, where do we go from here? What are our objectives in Syria? What is the strategy? And the short answer is this: At this point, there seems to be no strategy. A pinpoint missile strike is not a strategy. That is a problem for the people of Syria and it is part of a troubling pattern from the White House.

In 100 short days, the administration has escalated tensions with North Korea with reckless saber-rattling, gone hot and cold on China, cozied up to Putin, and caused diplomatic embarrassment for some of our closest allies. At the same time, most top State Department posts remain vacant and the expertise of our diplomats is clearly being ignored. You cannot fly by the seat of your pants when it comes to foreign policy.

On the global stage, policy by improvisation confuses our friends and tees up opportunities for our adversaries. For example, I am convinced that the administration's reversal on a long-held policy of removing Assad emboldened him to carry out the sarin gas attack in the first place.

If indeed there is a strategy, Congress has been kept in the dark. We were told that the administration would soon present us with its plan. That has not happened.

I think back to the 2011 strike in Libya, which also took place during a recess, and there was a lot of criticism for that, but the week Congress returned, Secretary Clinton, Secretary Gates, Chair of the Joint Chiefs Mullen, and DNI Clapper were all here on Capitol Hill telling lawmakers about the path forward. Whether we agreed with it or didn't agree with it, we at least learned about it. So far, no such briefing has been scheduled on Syria. And of course, no administration witnesses are testifying before us today because so few senior State Department officials are in place.

So while we wait for the administration to draw up a strategy, there are a few things that the President and his team should bear in mind. First, military action alone will not solve the crisis in Syria. Only a political transition, one that removes Assad from power, will put the Syrian people on the path toward rebuilding and re-charting the course for their country's future. We need the means to help push that process forward.

My bill that I introduced with Chairman Royce, the Caesar Syria Civilian Protection Act, would provide some of those tools to pressure Assad and his patrons in Moscow and Tehran. The House passed the bill unanimously last year and I am grateful to Chairman Royce for planning to mark up this legislation again next week.

We also need senior diplomats in place who can drive the policies that will lead to a solution. It is nearly May. The President has only just announced his pick for Deputy Secretary of State and he hasn't even nominated an Under Secretary for Political Affairs, or Assistant Secretary for Near Eastern Affairs. And rather than working to fill these vacancies as quickly as possible, the administration, instead, seems intent on slashing the resources needed to conduct effective diplomacy. We learned about that at the last hearing we had.

Second, there must be no further American military action in Syria without congressional say-so. The 60-day War Powers Resolution clock started ticking when President Trump notified Congress of the missile strike. The President must come to Congress if the Syria strategy includes military involvement. No matter anyone's view of how we should grapple with this problem, Congress' voice must be heard and we will not simply give this administration or any administration a blank check.

For now, I will keep pushing the administration for answers and pressing for a strategy that will advance a political solution, get Assad out of power, and end the suffering of the Syrian people.

I am grateful to our witnesses for sharing their views on what such a strategy looks like and I yield back the balance of my time.

Chairman ROYCE. Thank you, Mr. Engel. We did pass our bill out of this committee and out of the House last year. We are going to have an opportunity, in light of events—we couldn't get it out of the Senate last year but we are going to try to get it out of the Senate this year.

Mr. ENGEL. Thank you, Mr. Chairman and, as usual, your help was invaluable.

Chairman ROYCE. Thank you, Mr. Engel.

And now this morning we are pleased to be joined by a distinguished panel. Mr. Mike Singh is the managing director of the Washington Institute for Near East Policy and previously he served at the White House, where he oversaw the Middle East policy from 2005 to 2008.

And we have Mr. Charles Lister. He is a Senior Fellow at the Middle East Initiative. Previously, Mr. Lister was a visiting fellow at the Brookings Institution. He has been deeply focused on Syria policy for some time.

Dr. Dafna Rand is an adjunct professor at the National Defense University. Previously, she served as the Deputy Assistant Secretary of State in the Bureau for Democracy, Human Rights, and Labor.

So without objection, our witnesses' full prepared statements are going to be made part of the record and members here will have 5 calendar days to submit any statements as well, or any questions of you, or any extraneous materials for the record.

And so, Mr. Singh, this always works best if you could summarize your remarks and we will begin with you.

STATEMENT OF MR. MICHAEL SINGH, LANE-SWIG SENIOR FELLOW, MANAGING DIRECTOR, THE WASHINGTON INSTITUTE FOR NEAR EAST POLICY

Mr. SINGH. Mr. Chairman, Ranking Member Engel, members of the committee, thank you for having me here and thank you for your hard work on this issue.

Our past efforts to resolve or contain the conflict in Syria did not succeed; far from it. It is not now a civil war but a regional conflict that has drawn in Syria's neighbors and has had broad geopolitical ramifications beyond, including terrorism, and a refugee crisis in Europe, and political turbulence throughout the West.

Our problem in Syria is not simply an ISIS problem but runs much deeper and I want to talk about those broader ramifications. The Trump administration's start, I agree with both of you, has been promising. The April 7th strike was decisive and it served a clear, if narrow, interest in deterring the use of chemical weapons and enhancing our military credibility in Syria. But devising our broader Syria policy will be much more complicated and will require a similarly clear understanding of our interests and objectives and the development of options to advance them. And I think we need to begin with a quick assessment of the situation, which will reveal just how much the conflict has broiled the regional politics.

This is not, in fact, a single conflict but it is playing out over I would say four distinct zones. Each one of those zones has different internal and external actors involved. So for example, in western Syria, both Iran and Russia are defending the Assad regime's remaining territory, which is stronger, but for different reasons. Iran seeks to preserve Syria as a channel for the projection of power into the Levant; whereas, Russia I think wants to reassert a global role, thwart American aims in Syria, and preserve and expand its influence in the Middle East.

Turkey, for its part, has long advocated that the Assad regime—that Assad, himself, should step aside. But increasingly, Ankara is focused on preventing the aggrandizement of the Kurds. And its chief aims now seem to be preventing the establishment of a continuous Kurdish territory along the Syrian side of the Turkish border and preventing the United States from providing heavy weapons and training to the Kurds and their Arab partners in the SDF, the Syrian Democratic Forces.

If we look at Israel, Israel, for its part, is alarmed at the possibility of Iran and Hezbollah establishing a presence along the Golan Heights and very wary about what seems to be an emerging Russia-Iran-Hezbollah axis.

And then finally, Jordan, our other good partner in this region, worries about new refugee flows. It is already dealing with almost a million refugees, as well as the ISIS and Iranian presence on its northwestern border.

It is an enormously complex situation and I think we need to avoid framing our policy as an effort to sort of solve Syria, as it were, in one fell swoop or one neat package. Instead, we need to focus on setting discrete objectives that will protect our interests and I recommend three in particular.

First, I think we need to seek to prevent the Syrian conflict from further destabilizing the region. It could get worse, as bad as it is now in this region. So in western Syria, including the Idlib region, where the fight is increasingly between the Assad regime and its backers on the one hand and a jihadist-dominated opposition on the other, I think our chief concern needs to be for the millions of civilians who are caught in the middle of that fight.

So, we should continue providing humanitarian relief—we have provided more than any other country so far—providing escape routes for those civilians. But I think we also need to make clear, building on the April 7th strike, that further atrocities against civilians by Assad, and by his backers, could prompt a further use of force. I think that credible military threat needs to be there.

In southern Syria, we need to support our allies Israel and Jordan as they seek to prevent the conflict from spilling over their borders and as they seek to push ISIS back from their borders.

And then in northern Syria, where we have recently had this Turkish bombing of Kurdish positions, I think our chief aim needs to be to calm those Turkish-Kurdish tensions, urging Ankara to not engage in any more uncoordinated bombing but also urging the Syrian Kurds, the YPG, to sever their ties with the PKK, which is a terrorist group and where Turkey has a legitimate concern.

And as we plan Raqqa's liberation, I think we need to aim, ideally, to keep local Arab forces up front and to involve both the Turks and Kurds to the extent we can in the operation, rather than choosing one or the other in a way that will unbalance the politics there.

I think we also need to consider modestly increasing our own troop commitment, as we have in northern Iraq, so that we can play an effective coordinating role between those various forces.

Our second objective, I think, should be to push back on Iran and prevent it from using the Syrian conflict to expand its power. Iran is deeply entrenched in western Syria but it shouldn't get a free pass for its use of foreign fighters and its support for the Assad regime. And we need to keep up the pressure on Iran and Iranian entities that are involved in this effort. And now is the time also to ramp up the pressure on Hezbollah and to renew our support for the Government of Lebanon, which is deeply involved in this issue as well.

And then finally, we need to work with Israel and Jordan to ensure that Iran and its proxies don't establish a new front along the Golan Heights that I think would inflame tensions in this region for years to come.

Finally, thirdly, and quickly, our third objective needs to be to ensure that ISIS and al-Qaeda are denied safe haven after Raqqa's liberation so they can't return, so we are not dealing with this problem yet again in the coming years.

So the training and equipment we provide those local partners I think needs to be oriented not just toward defeating ISIS, not just that near-term goal, but also providing security for the local population afterwards. And we shouldn't just support security forces. We need to support local civil society who can help with the governance and rebuilding of eastern Syria.

I think both of these efforts will require international assistance and I think, to the extent we can, we should push our Arab allies to get involved in that effort, rather than having this be a U.S.-only effort.

Just in closing, members of the committee, it is critical that we defeat ISIS but how we go about defeating ISIS and how we pursue our other aims in Syria are going to have lasting ramifications for the geopolitics of the Middle East and for our own security.

Thank you.

[The prepared statement of Mr. Singh follows:]

Syria After the Missile Strikes: Policy Options

Michael Singh
Lane-Swig Senior Fellow and Managing Director,
The Washington Institute for Near East Policy

Testimony submitted to the House Foreign Affairs Committee
April 27, 2017

Mr. Chairman, Ranking Member Engel, and members of the committee, thank you for this opportunity to testify on American policy in Syria. This is rightly a topic of renewed attention in the aftermath of the April 7 cruise missile strike on Shayrat airfield, which came in response to the horrific use of chemical weapons by the Assad regime against the population of Khan Sheikhoun.

At first glance, there seems to be a tragic repetitiveness to the conflict in Syria—a drumbeat of bombings, battles, and refugee flows punctuated now and then by some new, more extreme outrage perpetrated by the Assad regime, ISIS, or another group. The unrelenting nature of this conflict not only threatens to desensitize us to the tragedies unfolding daily in Syria, but to mask the war's fundamental transformation from 2011 to today.

The Syria conflict began as a peaceful protest that was brutally suppressed, with an increasingly illegitimate regime fighting its people while creating the conditions for the development of an extremist opposition, albeit one which served as a useful foil for the regime. The United States and others long hoped to contain this conflict, but failed utterly; it is now a regional conflagration whose geopolitical ramifications have been felt far beyond the Middle East. One can draw a straight line from the conflict in Syria to the rise of ISIS, which prospered in the vacuum left by the Syrian state's decay; to Russia's reassertion of its power in the Middle East; to the refugee crisis in Europe and the Middle East; to the political turbulence which played a role in the British decision to leave the EU and continues to roil European politics today.

Our relative neglect of the Syria conflict has thus not served our interests, but has set them back in the Middle East and beyond. Nor has it spared us the expenditure of resources—the U.S. has provided at least $6.5 billion in humanitarian aid to Syrians (more than any other country), provided at least $400 million in aid to the Syrian opposition, and spent billions of dollars more on the campaign against ISIS in Syria.[1]

Those who defend American policy in Syria over the last eight years must depend on the non-falsifiable claim that whatever the costs of inaction, a more assertive policy would have been worse. The Trump administration has started out on the right foot by rejecting this approach and acting decisively in service of a clear U.S. interest. I believe the April 7 cruise missile strikes in response to the Assad regime's use of chemical weapons stand a good chance of deterring the

---

[1] These figures are drawn from "Armed Conflict in Syria: Overview and U.S. Response," Congressional Research Service, April 7, 2017, https://fas.org/sgp/crs/mideast/RL33487.pdf.

further use of CW in Syria and reinforcing more broadly the international norm against the use of such weapons, which appears to have been the administration's narrow intent.

Devising and executing our broader policy in Syria will be more complex, but will benefit from a similarly clear assessment of U.S. interests and objectives and the development of options to advance them. In doing so, we cannot afford to focus narrowly on one or another aspect of the conflict, such as defeating ISIS. Instead, we will need to consider how the policy choices we and others make in Syria will impact the geopolitical landscape in the Middle East and beyond in the future. That will be the focus of my testimony.

BACKGROUND

The war in Syria today is not a single conflict, but comprises multiple arenas, which are not wholly distinct but overlap with one another:

- First, western Syria, where the regime, supported by Russia, Iran, and Iranian proxies like Hezbollah, are fighting an opposition dominated by jihadist groups, primarily Hayat Tahrir al-Sham (which includes the former Jabhat al-Nusra). This fighting is currently most intense around Idlib. Millions of Syrian civilians, including internally displaced persons from other areas such as Aleppo, are caught in it. It is this region that includes Khan Sheikhoun, which was the target of Assad's chemical attack.

- Second, northern Syria, where Turkish-backed and Kurdish forces have both clashed with ISIS, in close proximity to Syrian regime and Russian forces, as they jostle for position. Turkish-backed forces maintain a triangle of territory including the towns of Jarabulus and al-Bab, in large part to prevent Syrian Kurdish (YPG) forces from linking territory they control in northwestern Syria around Afrin with the territory they control in the country's northeast stretching from Manbij to Qamishli, and thereby consolidating control of the entire Syrian-Turkish border area. This has in turn strengthened the incentive for the YPG to cooperate with regime and Russian forces, which control the area south of al-Bab and east of Aleppo, which forms an alternate land route between the Kurdish areas.

- Third, southern Syria. This area is contested by the Syrian regime, opposition groups, and ISIS. While it has generally been quieter of late than other areas, it is of particular strategic importance to two of our closest regional allies, Israel and Jordan.

- Fourth, eastern Syria, which along with a swath of central Syria around Palmyra remains in the hands of ISIS. ISIS' territory has slowly eroded thanks to coalition air strikes in conjunction with a ground campaign being waged largely by the Syrian Democratic Forces (SDF), which includes both the Kurdish YPG militia and local Arab elements.

Each of these conflicts has drawn in various actors from inside and outside Syria. These include the following (NB—Because this testimony focuses on the regional geopolitics of the conflict, only external actors are listed; this is not intended to downplay the central role of Syrian actors in the conflict and its resolution):

- Iran—Arguably the most significant outside actor in Syria, Iran has reportedly provided the Assad regime with tens of thousands[2] of fighters, arms, training, and other forms of support. While most of the Iranian-backed forces in Syria are proxies—most notably

---

[2] Majid Raided as quoted in Melissa Dalton, Testimony Before the House Foreign Affairs Committee, February 14, 2017.

Hezbollah but also Iraq, Afghan, and Pakistani Shia militants—numerous IRGC personnel, including high-ranking officers, have been killed in Syria and other Iranian security agencies have reportedly been involved.

Iran's involvement has been focused not on fighting ISIS, but on fighting opposition forces in western Syria, leading one to surmise that its objective is to defend the Assad regime. Ensuring Assad's survival is vital to Iran's effort to project power into the Levant against U.S. allies, primarily Israel. Were Assad to fall, Iran's channels to Hezbollah and other terrorist groups could be disrupted, and Iranian forces would not likely enjoy the freedom of action they long have had in Syria.

Iran's involvement in Syria has led to several concerning developments. While the IRGC and its proxies such as Hezbollah had typically engaged in insurgency in the past, their defense of the Assad regime has forced a shift to counter-insurgency. Whether this leads to overextension or aggrandizement is an open question, but there is evidence that their experience in Syria has increased their capacity for conventional operations.[3]

In addition, the Syria conflict appears to have cemented the Russia-Iran alliance, as vividly demonstrated by Russia's use of an Iranian airbase. It should be noted that sanctions barring the sale of conventional arms systems to Iran will lapse in 2020 as a result of the nuclear deal or Joint Comprehensive Plan of Action (JCPOA), opening further possibilities for conventional military cooperation between Russia, Iran, and Iran's proxies.

Finally, while Iran has thus far been focused on western Syria, one cannot dismiss the possibility that after the liberation of Mosul, Iraqi Shia militias beholden to Iran will seek to become involved in eastern Syria.

- Russia—While Russia's footprint in Syria has been smaller than Iran's, it has played no less decisive a role in safeguarding the Assad regime. With a relatively small (and thus perhaps sustainable) intervention, Russia arguably saved the Assad regime from severe contraction or destruction in late 2015 and enabled it to reverse some territorial losses, providing the air power to complement Iran's efforts on the ground.

  Russia, which like Iran has operated chiefly in western Syria rather than against ISIS, also aims to defend the Assad regime but for reasons which are different from Tehran's. It is perhaps the clearest case of what seems to be a global effort by Russian President Putin to restore Russia's status as a great power, in a place that was the last bastion of Russian influence in the region. Moscow likely also aims simply to thwart U.S. ambitions, in response to what it sees as U.S. efforts at regime change in Iraq, Libya, and elsewhere. Russian officials routinely claim that their purpose is to fight ISIS and that they have no special attachment to Assad himself, but neither assertion is borne out by Russian actions.

  Russia's intervention has had implications for the freedom of action of other forces. The U.S. cannot contemplate military action in Syria or the surrounding region without taking Russian air defenses into account, though their impact should not be exaggerated. And any action Israel contemplates in Lebanon or Syria also depends to some extent on Russian forbearance.

- Turkey—Ankara is a partner in U.S. efforts in Syria, providing access to the Incirlik air base and taking in millions of Syrian refugees. Turkey has long insisted that Assad

[3] See Genevieve Casagrande, "How Iran Is Learning from Russia in Syria," Institute for the Study of War (http://www.understandingwar.org/backgrounder/how-iran-learning-russia-syria) for more on this topic.

should step aside, but in recent months its chief concern in Syria appears to have been the territorial expansion of the Syrian Kurds, whom Turkey considers to be in league with the PKK terrorist group. As noted above, in 2016 (and continuing into 2017), Turkish-backed forces seized a swath of territory along the Syrian-Turkish border to prevent the YPG from linking its territories around Afrin with the area it holds in the east between Manbij and Qamishli. Turkey is likely to remain in control of this territory for the foreseeable future. While much was made of a softening of Russian-Turkish relations last year, the tensions between Moscow and Ankara over Syria are likely to persist, especially if links between Russia and the YPG deepen.

Turkey's concerns about the aggrandizement of the YPG has complicated the US-led campaign to oust ISIS from Raqqa, as the YPG-dominated SDF was seen as the likeliest candidate to lead that effort. The SDF-led "Euphrates Wrath" operation has been clearing territories around Raqqa in anticipation of the city's eventual liberation, while at the same time Turkish-backed opposition forces have stated their intention to roll back both ISIS and the YPG in the same area. Maintaining good relations with Turkey while mounting an effective campaign against ISIS in Raqqa has thus proven a conundrum for the U.S. and its coalition allies.

- Jordan—Amman's chief concerns in Syria are fourfold. First is the flow of refugees from Syria into Jordan, which already hosts nearly a million of them. Coalition operations in Raqqa and western Iraq, or renewed fighting in southern Syria, could trigger another outflow of refugees to Jordan. Second is the possibility of further ISIS attacks against Jordan, beyond the border (although until now all the major terrorist attacks that have occurred in the kingdom have been perpetrated by radicalized Jordanian nationals). Third is the outbreak of renewed fighting near Jordan's borders, whether between the Syrian regime and opposition or Israel and Iranian-backed forces, which could have dire consequences for Jordan's own security. Finally, Jordan seeks to prevent Iran and Hezbollah from establishing a base of operations along its northern border, which could be a destabilizing factor after the war eventually ends. To safeguard these interests, Jordan has been practical, seeking to maintain constructive relations with the Assad regime and Russia in recent months. Jordan has also reportedly been conducting, along with other anti-ISIS coalition forces, air and ground operations in southwest Syria, targeting ISIS and Al-Qaida militants.

- Israel—Israel's concerns in Syria appear to be threefold. The first is deterring any attacks from Syria into Israeli territory, regardless of the source. To this end, Israel has responded proportionately to projectiles originating in Syria and striking Israel, and these exchanges have thus far not escalated. Second, Israel is concerned about the possibility of Iranian and Iranian-backed forces, such as the IRGC and Hezbollah, establishing a new front with Israel on the Golan Heights. In fact, the Institute for the Study of War indicates that these groups have already established positions close to the northern edge of the Golan.[4] Third, Israel is concerned about the emerging alliance between Iran, Hezbollah, and Russia, which if it advances could severely undermine Israel's qualitative military edge and security broadly. Israel also has a longstanding interest in preventing the transfer of advanced weaponry to Hezbollah via Syrian territory, and has reportedly conducted strikes inside both Syria and Lebanon to halt such transfers.

---

[4] See "Posture of Syrian Regime and Allies: March 21, 2017," Institute for the Study of War, http://www.understandingwar.org/sites/default/files/Regime%20-%20Iranian%20Posture%20MAR%202017_2.pdf.

- Others—Many other outside actors have interests and limited involvement in the Syrian conflict. The Gulf states have provided support to Syrian opposition groups in an effort to counter Iranian regional influence, but over time their focus has largely shifted to the Yemen conflict, which poses a more direct threat to the Arabian peninsula. Iraq is closer to Syria than other Gulf Arab states, and the U.S. should use its leverage with Baghdad—which presumably is stronger now than it will be in the future—to ensure that Iraqi Shia militias do not enter the fray with fellow Iranian-backed forces in Syria after Mosul's liberation.

Europe is arguably more threatened by the Syrian conflict than is the U.S., given the far larger number of refugees who have fled to Europe and the more significant ISIS presence there. However, the involvement of European states in the Syria conflict has been limited so far. Finally, China has had a small role in the conflict, reportedly cooperating with the Syrian regime on intelligence matters as a result of Chinese nationals traveling to fight with ISIS, and supporting Russian efforts to block UN Security Council action on Syria until Beijing's recent absention on a draft resolution condemning the Khan Sheikhoun attack. All of these actors are to some extent possible partners for the United States in Syria.

IMPLICATIONS FOR U.S. POLICY

As the Trump administration crafts its policy toward Syria, it will need to take as a starting point today's reality. This might seem obvious, but there is a temptation in policymaking to use current policy to correct for past errors. But whatever one's criticisms of President Obama's approach to Syria, the mistakes of 2011, 2013, and 2015 cannot be revisited, and the policy recommendations made then must be put aside in favor of ones suited to the present situation.

Today's realities are stark. As noted above, Syria is fragmented. Reunifying Syria does not, for the time being, appear to be within the power of any Syrian or outside actor, whether the Assad regime or the opposition. While it is still right to insist that Assad is illegitimate and should step aside, it is important to recognize that in reality his government no longer rules the majority of Syria.

Russia and Iran are deeply entrenched in western Syria, and entangled with one another. While their interests are not the same, as noted above, they depend operationally on one another to advance their respective interests, and thus will be difficult to split. In addition, Russia's presence constricts American freedom of action not just against Assad, but also to a large extent against Iranian and Iranian-backed forces, given their close coordination. However, this does not mean splitting Russia and Iran, or at least limiting the extent of their alliance, should not remain a long-term U.S. objective in Syria. Nor do the constraints on our freedom of action render us impotent; demonstrating this was one of the most important consequences of the U.S. cruise missile strike on April 7.

In addition, the anti-ISIS campaign has already accomplished much of what it ultimately will. The group's territory has been steadily shrinking, and while it may break out in minor ways, it is unlikely a serious threat to seize territory on a significant scale in Syria or Iraq given our current policy. The coalition must still finish the job, but we should be realistic about the extent of the impact Raqqa's liberation will have on the Syria conflict at this stage, and we should already be planning for the next phase of that conflict.

Finally, in designing a Syria policy, the Trump administration should resist "solutionism." The roots of the conflicts in Syria run very deep; the United States will not and should not "solve"

Syria, even if we expend vast resources in the attempt. Instead, the U.S. should determine what objectives are necessary to advance our vital interests, and devise strategies and policies to accomplish them.

These objectives should include the following:

1. *Prevent the Syria conflict from further destabilizing the region.* While the fighting in Syria has already drawn in numerous regional actors and had a serious economic and security impact on the region, it could get worse yet. The U.S. should consider steps that independently stabilize each of the conflict's areas of fighting, and be modest about any grand diplomatic effort to settle them all at once.

    a. Around Idlib, American options are limited given that both sides—the Assad regime and its Russian and Iranian partners on the one hand, and jihadist groups such as Hayat Tahrir al-Sham on the other—are anathema to the U.S. Rather than involving ourselves in the fighting, the U.S. should, in conjunction with our European allies, focus on the protection of civilians and the provision of humanitarian relief. Following up on the April 7 strike and to deter Assad and Russia primarily, the U.S. should warn that we and our allies reserve the right to respond with force to atrocities committed against civilians.

    b. In southern Syria, the U.S. should urge Russia to refrain from large-scale bombing in order to prevent the region's further destabilization. The U.S. should continue to aid Jordan, Israel, and/or non-jihadist opposition forces as needed with any operations to push ISIS, other jihadist groups, or Iranian-backed groups away from their borders. Preparation for Raqqa's liberation should include provision for refugees within Syria, lest they flee for Jordan.

    c. In northern and eastern Syria, the U.S. should lead a diplomatic effort to calm tensions between Turkey and the Syrian Kurds. Washington should seek Kurdish guarantees that they will not seek to extend their territory further, and Turkish pledges to respect core Kurdish territory in Syria. Because of Turkey's concerns about the U.S. provision of heavy weapons and training to the SDF, and local Arab concerns about Kurdish influence, the U.S. should seek to involve both Turkish-backed and SDF forces in any Raqqa operation. In addition, we should consider greater involvement by U.S., European, and Arab forces to minimize the roles of both Turkey and the Syrian Kurds.[5] Assad, Iranian and Iranian-backed forces, and Russia should be excluded from any effort to liberate Raqqa.

    d. Rather than pursuing a diplomatic settlement in the manner of the Obama Administration, the Trump administration should withhold U.S. endorsement from any diplomatic process that does not require Assad to step aside and hold him to account. U.S. acquiescence is valuable to Russia and Iran, and it should not be given away freely, especially because they have demonstrated little ability or will to guarantee Assad's adherence to agreements. This should not rule out local ceasefires, however.

    e. The U.S. should create, as CSIS' Melissa Dalton has suggested, a "U.S.-led multilateral forum in which tensions and conflicting objectives can be addressed with

---

[5] For a fuller treatment of this issue, see testimony by Ambassador James F. Jeffrey to the Senate Foreign Relations Committee, February 7, 2017.

key allies and partners on the Syria problem set (including Turkey, Israel, Jordan, and the Gulf partners)."[6]

2. *Limit Iran's projection of power and the aggrandizement of Iranian-backed forces.* One of the most dangerous flash points in the Middle East remains southern Lebanon, as a result of the massive armaments and extensive training that Iran has provided to Hezbollah for the purpose of threatening Israel. It should be our objective not only to prevent the growth of this threat, but to counter Iran across the Levant through the following actions.

   a. The U.S. should treat Iranian-backed forces as any other foreign fighters, and insist that others do so as well; any internationally recognized settlement to the conflict in Syria should require Iran to withdraw its forces and its proxies from the country. Similarly, any discussion of terrorist groups in Syria should address not only Sunni, but Shia terrorist groups such as Hezbollah as well.

   b. The U.S. should warn Iran that it reserves the right to use force, or back Israel's use of force, against any IRGC or Hezbollah positions established in proximity to the Israeli or Jordanian borders.

   c. The U.S. should aggressively target Iranian entities that violate sanctions on Syria, and block any aircraft sales to Iran unless the recipient airlines can positively demonstrate that they are not involved in ferrying fighters or materiel to Syria. In addition, the U.S. should ramp up sanctions and other pressure on Hezbollah and its supporters in Lebanon and elsewhere.

   d. The Trump administration should work with the Iraqi government to prevent the travel of Shia militias from Iraq to Syria following the liberation of Mosul.

   e. The U.S. should reinvigorate efforts, largely dropped by the Obama administration, to support Lebanon's sovereignty, to ensure that it is not subsumed into western Syria should Syria's fragmentation persist.

3. *Deny safe haven to jihadist groups including ISIS and Al-Qaida and prevent the return of ISIS after Raqqa's liberation.* Perhaps the most significant challenge surrounding Raqqa's liberation is what follows afterward. Unlike in Iraq, there is no established authority to whom the U.S. can pass the baton; one must instead be fostered.

   a. Any international train-and-equip mission for local Arab forces in eastern Syria should emphasize not only the urban warfare that will be required to oust ISIS from Raqqa, but the follow-on operations that will be required to provide security for the local population and prevent ISIS' return or the emerge of Al-Qaida.

   b. Security assistance should be paired with aid to civil society organizations – not only those providing humanitarian relief, but also ones which can help restore law, order, and services in liberated areas.

   c. The role of both the Kurds and the Turks in eastern Syria should be limited, and Arab states, and to a lesser extent European forces, should instead be encouraged to play a role, especially in counter-terrorism.

---

[6] Dalton.

OUTCOMES

The ideal outcome in Syria from the point of view of American interests is a unified Syria with a pro-Western, pluralistic government. This is perhaps the least likely outcome in the foreseeable future, however, given the country's increasing fragmentation and demographic polarization and the failure of diplomatic efforts to date. Equally unrealistic is an outcome in which the Assad regime reasserts control over all of Syria; it lacks the capacity to do so, and even if it had those capabilities, its rule would trigger continued violent resistance from Syrians who reject Assad's legitimacy. More realistic, perhaps, is a federal Syria comprised of semi-autonomous regions. But few actors in Syria or the region favor such an outcome, and they could be expected to resist it long after it had become a reality. The best approach for the United States is to pursue our interests while promoting stability in each of the conflict's disparate arenas, gradually expanding our zone of influence with an eye toward a broader diplomatic settlement down the road.

Chairman ROYCE. Thank you.

Mr. Lister.

STATEMENT OF MR. CHARLES LISTER, SENIOR FELLOW, MIDDLE EAST INSTITUTE

Mr. LISTER. Chairman Royce, Ranking Member Engel, members of the committee, thank you for inviting me here today to testify on this very important subject.

Today, the Assad regime has sat more comfortably in Damascus than at any point since the start of the crisis in early 2011. Its recent use of chemical weapons is almost certainly a result of that confidence. However, if anyone believes that Assad is now the key to stabilizing Syria, they are sorely mistaken. Assad will never be capable of putting Syria back together again. Not only does his continued survival represent radicalization gold dust but it also fuels the continued exodus of his own population.

So what now? Clearly, the status quo is not working. Determined U.S. leadership backed up by a credible threat of force and a holistic underpinning strategy represents the best opportunity to strongarm actors into a phase of meaningful de-escalation, out of which a durable negotiation process may eventually result.

Punitive strikes and other assertive acts of diplomacy will be inevitable but if anything is now clear, it is that we have far more freedom of action in Syria than the previous administration was ever willing to admit. Opponents of limited U.S. intervention, who long and confidently pronounced the inevitability of conflict of Russia, are now faced with the reality that Russia failed to lift a finger when American missiles careened toward Assad regime targets.

The first step to developing a more effective Syria policy is to acknowledge that Syria can be divided into dozens of unique semicontained conflicts and that countering terrorism isn't enough to protect our interests. We need a holistic strategy that treats all of Syria's various symptoms as interlinked components of one big root cause.

The fight against ISIS in Syria has made significant progress but we must acknowledge the challenges ahead and the disadvantageous effects of certain aspects of our strategy. The big looming challenge is the fight for Raqqa and the issue at hand is who our local partners are for that battle. The favored status given thus far to the Kurdish YPG has created serious issues with our NATO ally Turkey, which claims the YPG is affiliated to the PKK, a movement that we, ourselves, consider a terrorist organization. In fact, the YPG's direct affiliation with the PKK was publicly acknowledge repeatedly by our very own National Counterterrorism Center, until we began working with the group in 2014.

We need Turkey as a constructive partner. Laudable efforts have been undertaken to recruit Arabs to fight alongside the YPG but the YPG retains overwhelming influence over tactics, strategy, and outcomes. The YPG also maintains ambiguous relations with the Assad regime. Already, territory captured from ISIS thanks to intensive U.S. assistance has been handed back to the Assad regime and to Russia. A YPG-led victory in Raqqa would almost certainly lead to a similar result, which would embolden extremists and create the conditions for new conflict.

We do not need to rush Raqqa and it is not at all clear that our existing partners are capable of taking the city. Instead, we should use our influence with Turkey to push for a ceasefire with the PKK, which may help ease tensions with the YPG in Syria. As part of a package deal, we could then offer to include a portion of Turkey's anti-Assad forces, most of which are already vetted by the CIA and CENTCOM, into a broader Raqqa offensive. This would be a similar arrangement to that which we worked out for Mosul in Iraq.

While our eyes have been firmly fixed on ISIS, al-Qaeda has thrived in Syria. It sought to deeply embed itself into Syria's broad opposition movement. It has adapted its narrative to fit that of much of the opposition and it studiously avoided many of the extremist practices typically associated with al-Qaeda. This use of what I call controlled pragmatism is in marked difference from ISIS and means that countering al-Qaeda in Syria necessitates the use of a very different toolkit. This is a struggle defined by a competition for narrative victory. Six years of violence and no determined international action to stop it has provided al-Qaeda with an increasingly pliable population and an opportunity to exploit its principle advantage, its power in battle. Determined action to protect civilians and deter regime war crimes, paired with a substantial reduction in conflict would represent a serious threat to al-Qaeda.

However, greater pressure is needed on its most important area of operations, the Province of Idlib. This is a problem that only Turkey is well-placed to tackle, though it would require substantial U.S. support. Here, we would seek to replicate Turkey's actions against ISIS and the YPG north of Aleppo to create a reality on the ground of steadily expanding ink spots. In Aleppo, those ink spots have since turned into de facto safe zones from which adversaries were defeated, al-Qaeda fled, reconstruction has now re-begun, refugees are returning, moderate rebel groups are being trained, and police are taking over from armed groups. The opposition interim government now plans to establish offices in this area.

Beyond countering terrorism, there is no immediate opening for a nationwide settlement. As such, we should pursue an interim solution, imposing calm to distinct geographic zones. Creating zones of calm along Syria's borders will assist an eventual process of refugee resettlement and constrain or even stop the flow of weapons and money intended for armed activities. It would give opposition territories the opportunity to begin governance and service provision free from aerial bombing and it will allow some level of interim reconstruction to begin.

Creating multiple facts on the ground will also represent a considerable source of pressure on Assad and may eventually allow for a meaningful initiation of negotiations. For this reason, the United States would need to pursue an intensive track of bilateral negotiations with Russia throughout the lead-up to and as these zones of calm take form.

For this reason, America and its allies must be prepared for enforcement. Credible threats of punitive force can create meaningful diplomatic leverage but only when part of a clearly defined strategy.

Finally, this deterrence should encompass more than the use of internationally banned weapons. It is important for us to establish a moral equivalency. Conventional weapons are far more deadly than sarin gas. In fact, Assad's aerial bombing of his own population has killed at least 57 times as many people as the use of chemicals and banned chemical weapons. It should not be a matter of the murder weapon that defines whether murder is acceptable or not.

Thank you.

[The prepared statement of Mr. Lister follows:]

Written Testimony of Charles Lister
Senior Fellow, Middle East Institute
To the United States House Committee on Foreign Affairs
April 27, 2017

Hearing on "Syria After the Missile Strikes: Policy Options"

Mr. Chairman, Mr. Ranking Member, Members of the Committee:

First, thank you for providing me with this opportunity to speak to you today, and to address the situation in Syria and what policy options the United States might consider going forward.

Three weeks ago, the United States military fired 59 Tomahawk cruise missiles at Syria's Al-Shayrat airbase as a punitive response for the Syrian government's use of a Sarin-like nerve agent against a residential area of the town of Khan Sheikhoun three days earlier. This was a justified, proportionate and necessary response to a flagrant war crime, committed in full view of the world. Images and video footage showing men, women and children losing control of their muscles, succumbing to uncontrollable convulsions and then foaming from the mouth and nose shocked the world.

Whereas the United States' decision not to act in response to a similar attack in August 2013 that killed fifteen times as many people drew ire amongst allies and adversaries, the decision to act this time around was widely praised by U.S. partners near and far. Whereas the U.S. decision not to act in August 2013 was justified at the time by a Russian-facilitated deal to remove and destroy Syria's chemical weapons stockpile, events in Khan Sheikhoun demonstrated starkly that that deal had been a ruse. Israeli intelligence now assesses that Bashar al-Assad has secretly retained at least three tons of Sarin nerve agent, enough to kill many thousands more people, should he choose to do so. This was not much of a secret. Officials in the U.S. government and all of our principal allies have known as much for years.

For six years, U.S. policy on Syria has been characterized by lots of talk and very little action. For six years, U.S. policy on Syria has sought to convince our adversaries to behave through dialogue, hoping to facilitate some semblance of stability in Syria based on trust, when no such trust has existed. The results of pursuing dialogue with no muscle behind it are clear and horrifying: half a million Syrians dead and 11.5 million more either internally displaced or refugees. Syria's collapse into chaos assisted ISIS in its dramatic recovery, out of which it has declared a Caliphate and forced the international community to form one of the broadest military coalitions in history. Meanwhile, a globally weakened Al-Qaeda has used Syria to adapt and evolve its self-presentation and strategic objectives, so much so that many people in the region now see it as a credible resistance movement fighting the 'good fight.' As a result, America and its allies now face an Al-Qaeda with sources of genuine popularity, something ISIS never acquired.

The consistent deterioration of the situation in Syria has also brought us a huge refugee crisis, which itself is the result of the Assad regime's scorched earth tactics. The unprecedented refugee flows out of Syria witnessed in recent years have crippled America's strategic partners in the region and sparked countless social, economic and political crises throughout European NATO allies. Iran is also now more powerful than ever; its Revolutionary Guard Corps has evolved into a professional and capable expeditionary force exerting influence across all corners of the Middle East; Hezbollah is now more powerful than some small Eastern European militaries; and dozens of transnational Shia militias now roam across established state borders, acting expressly against our own interests.

The Syrian crisis is immensely complicated – I have spent virtually every single day since March 2011 trying my best to understand it. Despite this very clear complexity, one thing ought to be simple: the continued presence of Bashar al-Assad in Damascus as Syria's self-proclaimed President does *not* promise any semblance of hope for the country's future. In fact, his stalwart refusal to consider even basic political reform in 2011 and his embracing of an escalatory set of military measures to, in his words, "cleanse" his population of the enemy, now represents *the* root cause of virtually every terrible consequence of the conflict in Syria. Considering our preeminent fixation on the threat of terrorism since 9/11, we must acknowledge that the single biggest push and pull factor for both Al-Qaeda and ISIS in Syria, is the Assad regime's continued survival and the brutal violence it unleashes upon its people.

At no point in the last six years has the United States truly sought to address this root cause. Instead, we have switched from all talk and no action, to lots of talk and action to address symptoms. This is a containment strategy, not a solution. Nothing at all has got better in Syria through our pursuit of this approach and it is not unreasonable to suggest that nothing is likely to get better if we continue. Widespread perceptions of U.S. weakness and risk aversion have borne out clear consequences. But it is not too late.

Today, we meet in the seventh year of the conflict in Syria. Much has changed, particularly since Russia's military intervention in September 2015 – an act itself that was only possible because nobody believed the United States would prevent it. In April 2017, the Assad regime finds itself sat more comfortably in Damascus than at any point since the start of the crisis in the Spring of 2011. Its use of banned chemical weapons a few weeks ago is almost certainly a result of that confidence.

However, if anyone believes that Bashar al-Assad is now the key to stabilizing Syria, they have learned nothing from the country's recent history. Assad cannot and will never be capable of putting Syria back together again. Six years of mass murder, sectarian massacres, the industrialized use of torture and execution, the repeated use of chemical weapons, barrel bombs, ballistic missiles and more does not just represent extremist radicalization gold-dust, it is also clear and incontrovertible evidence that Bashar al-Assad has little to offer in terms of popular credibility or a promise of stability in Syria.

It is also important not to forget history. To claim that Bashar al-Assad was never our enemy would be to brush over his extraordinary and widely documented role in empowering ISIS's predecessor movements in Iraq, who fought against and killed American soldiers for years on end. As U.S. troops entered Iraq in March 2003, Assad's personally appointed Grand Mufti issued a fatwa declaring it religiously obligatory for all Muslims – male and female – to resist the invasion using any available means, including suicide bombing. Iraq's then foreign minister claimed 5,000 foreign fighters crossed into the country from Syria in the first 11 days of the invasion. Most of these were driven to the border on Syrian government buses, as Syrian border guards waved them across unchecked. According to captured Islamic State documents, more than 700 foreign jihadists crossed into Iraq from Syria through one town alone in a 12-month period between 2006-2007. Later in 2007, U.S. intelligence estimated that as much as 90% of Islamic State suicide bombers in Iraq had come through Syria – many flying into Aleppo or Damascus airports and then given free access to the Iraqi border. In mid-2009, the Syrian government's military intelligence service convened a meeting in the Syrian mountain town of Zabadani, in which Assad regime officials sat alongside leaders from the Islamic State and from Iraq's deposed Baath Party and planned a series of debilitating bombings aimed at crippling Prime Minister Nouri al-Maliki's standing in Baghdad. We know about this meeting only because Iraqi intelligence had a mole in the room, wearing a wire. Those attacks took place in August 2009 and left over 700 killed and wounded. It is quite possible that hundreds of American troops would still be alive today had it not been for Assad's explicit support for what was then known as the Islamic State in Iraq.

That tacit support for jihadists as a means of furthering Assad regime interests did not end in 2010, however. As men, women and children were taking to the streets in protest against Assad's dictatorial rule in the first half of 2011, Assad ordered the release of hundreds of imprisoned jihadists from jail. This was a cynical move to justify Assad's description of the opposition as radicals from Day One. While pro-democracy activists were being disappeared at night and arrested in the day, Al-Qaeda jihadists were being let out on amnesty. Two of the al-Nusra Front's seven founding members were amongst those released, as were at least 10 of its other senior leaders. Three of ISIS's most important leaders in Syria were also released, including the Emirs of Aleppo and Raqqa, the de facto capital of the Caliphate. As Syria's opposition movement gained steam later in 2011, Assad's personally appointed Grand Mufti threatened to unleash "martyrdom seekers" to Europe, should external powers intervene. Two Congress people have since met with this Grand Mufti.

In short, Bashar al-Assad – in both everything he has done and everything he represents – does not and should never represent what we consider to be an acceptable future for Syria and its people. It should also go without saying that the choice we face today is not and has never been a binary one between Assad and ISIS, as some have tried to claim. Syria remains a country of many communities and many perspectives. Of a population of roughly 23 million people, no more than 20,000 (0.09 percent) have chosen today to be members of Al Qaeda or ISIS. Therefore, U.S. policy is best served by securing a future for the remaining 99.91 percent. This is also not merely a matter of attending to resident Syrians inside Syria. Over 5 million Syrian citizens (roughly 22% of the population) are currently registered as refugees, residing outside of

Syria, while a further 6.3 million (roughly 27% of the population) are homeless and displaced inside the country. Those people require a voice too, in determining their country's future.

So what now? Clearly the status quo is not working. To call for a continuation of existing policy is to accept that Syria will be unstable for a decade or more, and the terrorist threat regionally and internationally will undoubtedly grow. Major foreign intervention in search of regime change, however, carries far too many risks and promises only further chaos. What is needed is a policy that sits in-between. Determined U.S. leadership backed up by the credible and now proven threat of force presents the best opportunity in years to strong-arm actors on the ground into a phase of meaningful de-escalation, out of which eventually, a durable negotiation process may result. This is, sadly, something the previous administration refused to accept. Repeated, well-meaning efforts to broker peace failed because that administration refused even to consider threatening the use of force. Every rhetorical threat given from an Obama podium effectively amounted to a further emboldening of the Assad regime's sense of impunity and its free hand to murder its people en masse.

Any path forward in Syria will be a long one. There are no quick fixes and there are unlikely to be quick interim results either. Setting Syria on a path towards stability will undoubtedly necessitate a further strengthening of the U.S. posture. More punitive military strikes and other assertive acts of diplomacy will be inevitable, but if anything is now clear, it is that the U.S. has more freedom of action in Syria than the Obama administration was ever willing to admit. Opponents of limited U.S. intervention who have long and confidently pronounced the inevitability of conflict with Russia are now faced with the reality that Moscow failed to lift a finger when American missiles careered toward Assad regime targets.

This is not to suggest that Russia plans to sit back and watch the United States threaten or undermine its proxy, Assad. Russia's seat on the U.N. Security Council and its conventional military assets make it appear to be the key *obstacle* to progress, but it may well end up being the key to moving *forward* in a better direction. For Russia, the Syrian issue remains something to be negotiated, though naturally it wants such negotiations to occur within a dynamic that better suits its negotiating position. In the past, we have come to the table with little leverage, because we refused to seek any. That is reversible, to an extent.

Beyond Russia though, Iran is arguably a far greater challenge and obstacle to progress. For Iran, the fate of Assad appears to be non-negotiable, at least within today's dynamics. Sustaining a friendly regime in Damascus is of existential importance to Tehran's regional strategy, particularly considering Hezbollah's near-total reliance on Iranian arms supplies through Syria, and Damascus in particular. Keeping Assad in place also secures Iranian hegemony through Tehran-Baghdad-Damascus-Beirut and into the Palestinian Territories. Beyond being a great victory for Iran, that also represents a major defeat to American interests and influence in the region. It also risks inflaming further, existing great power competition involving Iran, Saudi Arabia and Turkey.

Russia's intervention in Syria saved Assad from possible defeat, that is clear. However, the more secure Assad feels, the less he appears restrained by Russian instruction. In other words, Russia's leverage over Assad may be declining. This is also an issue of manpower. Russians closely acquainted with Syria decision-making and assessments in Moscow assess that Russia's key partner in Syria, the national Army, retains no more than 20,000 personnel who it believes to be sufficiently trained, offensively deployable and loyal for use in key operations. Iran on the other hand has key hands in Syrian paramilitary and foreign Shia militia forces that may now number 150,000 men at arms. Some of those groups are designated terrorist organizations, legally no different from al Qaeda or ISIS; others have become intrinsic components of the Assad regime's state apparatus. As one prominent Russian in Moscow recently told me in Europe, even Russia's own Spetsnaz special forces have come to respect one such Iran-backed terrorist group — Hezbollah — more than the Syrian Army itself.

Given this force imbalance, Russia has taken to deploying what it calls "military police" units to Syria, to hold important territory and to train new Syrian army conscripts. These "military police" forces have come from across Russia's North Caucasus region and reliable Russian sources inform me they are elite, counter-terrorism specialists. Russia is also coordinating the formation of new Syrian volunteer auxiliary forces, known as the 4th and 5th Legions. Gathering from recent publicity photographs, a sizeable majority of these volunteers are aged men, far from their fighting prime. Combined, these efforts and others appear to be Russian attempts at force multiplication, to shore up additional sources of leverage in Damascus.

As things stand today, Syria can be divided up into dozens of semi-contained conflicts, every one of which is individually unique. Assad may be more secure than ever, but he is a very long way from a full territorial re-conquest of his country. That objective may take a decade, or not even be possible at all. Despite this dissolution into multiple conflicts, the solution to Syria is not to be found in partition. In fact, that is one of the only issues that the opposition and the regime currently agree on. Despite the intensity and complexity of conflict, Syrians on both sides of the conflict still share a shared sense of Syrian identity. Although hard to see through the bullets and gas, this is a crucially important realization. Syria's non-jihadist opposition, as varied, complicated and imperfect as it is, remains a force of 80,000-100,000 heavily-armed men. A substantial majority of these men, and their sons, are not considering giving up their struggle anytime soon. That is also a crucially important realization. It will only be by addressing these kinds of realities that we will begin to define a meaningful policy.

The first step to developing a more effective Syria policy is to acknowledge that countering terrorism is not enough to protect our interests in the short or long-term. A holistic strategy is required that treats all the various symptoms as inter-linked components of a very big problem. The United States can choose to make big decisions and spend substantial amounts of resources now, or we can continue today's strategy and face virtual certainty of having to come back and do even more to try to fix an even greater problem several years from now. The word "unprecedented" is frequently used to describe problems emanating from Syria today. That is for a reason. We cannot hope to fix such issues by dipping our toes in the quagmire.

Counter-Terrorism: ISIS

The fight against ISIS in Syria has made significant progress, but it is important to acknowledge the challenges ahead and the disadvantageous knock-on effects of certain aspects of our strategy. The big challenge looming ahead is the fight for Raqqa and the major issue at hand is who our local partners are for that battle. Until now, the United States has demonstrated a clear preference for the Kurdish People's Protection Units (the YPG) and allied militias and tribes, collectively known as the Syrian Democratic Forces (SDF).

The favored status given to the YPG and its political wing, the Democratic Union Party (the PYD) has created serious issues with NATO ally Turkey, as it claims the PYD and YPG are affiliated to the Kurdistan Workers Party (the PKK), with whom it has fought a sustained war since the late-1970s. The United States has recognized the PKK as a designated terrorist organization since 1997. Turkey does have a point here. After all, the YPG was established by the brother of the PKK's God-like leader, Abdullah Ocalan, and the majority of the YPG's most senior and impactful leaders in Syria today owe their allegiance to the PKK's transnational leadership structure, known as the KCK. In fact, the United States government's very own National Counter-Terrorism Center accepted this much in its annual profiles of designated terrorist organizations, stating clearly in 2014 that the PYD was the "Syrian affiliate" of the PKK. Upon beginning our relationship with the PYD and YPG, however, that paragraph was removed from the NCTC profile in 2015 and 2016.

The United States needs Turkey to be a constructive partner on Syria's northern border, if we are to ever successfully defeat the terrorist threats emanating from there. As such, laudable efforts have been undertaken to recruit Arab tribes into the SDF, but contrary to much of the reporting on the issue, the YPG retains overwhelming influence over the SDF's tactics, strategy and outcomes. Moreover, for Arabs to join the SDF, the YPG precludes their inclusion by providing them with ideological training, in which certain revolutionary Marxist ideals are fused with the unique ideology developed by PKK leader Ocalan himself. Those who insufficiently buy into the PKK's ideology are said to receive little responsibility on the battlefield. The YPG does nothing to hide its hostility to Turkey either, including in the presence of American soldiers. The YPG also maintains ambiguous relations with the Assad regime. One strategically important town, Manbij, which was captured with U.S. military support, has since been effectively handed over to the Assad regime by the YPG. A YPG-led victory in Raqqa would almost certainly lead to a similar result, which itself would embolden ISIS and Al-Qaeda in a very big way and create the conditions for a further zone of complex conflict.

The United States does not need to rush our push to Raqqa. Doing so risks achieving the short-term objective – the city's capture – but securing groups like ISIS with an invaluable narrative victory. The United States should use its significant diplomatic leverage with Turkey to push for consideration of a ceasefire with the PKK inside Turkey, which may help ease tensions with the YPG across the border in Syria. As part of a package deal with Turkey, the United States could offer to include a select portion of its anti-Assad forces – the majority of which have already been vetted either by the CIA or by CENTCOM – into a broader offensive on Raqqa. This would be a similar arrangement to that worked out for Mosul, where zones of responsibility were pre-arranged between rival or competing factions.

Counter-Terrorism: Al-Qaeda

While our eyes have been fixed firmly on the threat posed by ISIS, Al-Qaeda's presence in Syria has thrived. Whereas ISIS has consistently sought to act alone and has aggressively avoided working with others, Al-Qaeda has sought to deeply embed itself into Syria's broad, opposition movement. It has constantly adapted its narrative to fit those of much of the opposition and it has studiously avoided many of the extremist practices typically associated with Al-Qaeda. This use of what I call "controlled pragmatism" has allowed it to methodically socialize more and more people into first accepting its presence within their midst, and then to supporting it. That many opposition Syrians – and indeed many people across the Middle East – see it in a different way than Al-Qaeda of the past, means that it has attracted a significant number of Syrian recruits who do not yet buy into the transnational jihadist ideal. Instead, they have merely chosen to join a popular group with a very successful track record on the battlefield.

This very marked difference from how ISIS has operated means that countering Al-Qaeda in Syria necessitates the use of a very different tool kit. In a sense, this is a struggle defined by a competition for narrative victory. Six years of brutal violence in Syria, paired with a total lack of determined international action to put a stop to it, has provided Al-Qaeda with an increasingly pliable population seemingly devoid of alternatives. Sustained levels of conflict have also given Al-Qaeda the opportunity to consistently exploit its principal advantage: its power in battle. Stronger international action aimed at protecting civilians and punishing regime war crimes, paired with a substantial reduction in conflict represents a very serious threat to Al-Qaeda. It was not a coincidence that the entirety of Syria's opposition welcomed and praised the recent cruise missile strikes and only Al-Qaeda issued a rebuke.

Taking away Al-Qaeda's narrative dominance can help deal with its popularity, which by extension, may give many desperate Syrians the confidence to embrace alternatives other than Al-Qaeda. Pursuing the abovementioned actions will also set into motion a chain of events that would likely lead to Al-Qaeda isolating itself as it acted in ways to protect its base. We have seen this happen before, on a much smaller scale.

Greater pressure, however, is needed on its most powerful area of operations: the province of Idlib. This is a problem that only Turkey is well placed to tackle, though it would require substantial U.S. support and protection. In August 2016, the Turkish military crossed into northern Aleppo's countryside alongside allied opposition groups to seek two objectives: the localized defeat of ISIS and the establishment of a buffer zone, preventing the YPG from sealing a contiguous swathe of territory. In so doing, Turkey catalyzed a total withdrawal of Al-Qaeda forces from northern Aleppo, as the group openly refused to cooperate with any foreign government or to align itself with U.S.-backed opposition forces, which Turkey was using.

As that zone of territory steadily expanded, it also grew into a de facto safe zone, as neither Russia nor the Assad regime dared fly over it and risk targeting Turkish troops. In the time since, this swathe of territory that now measures 110km by 60km, has received substantial sums of financial support for re-development and re-building. Tens of thousands of refugees have crossed from Turkey back into Syria and with Turkish pressure, populated areas are now being vacated by armed opposition groups and law and order is being assumed by Turkish trained Syrian civilian police forces. The area has also become home to at least 14 separate opposition military facilities, in which Turkish special forces are training Free Syrian Army affiliated groups for future operations. The U.S. recognized Syrian opposition Interim Government now plans to establish in-country offices in this area.

The evacuation of Al-Qaeda from northern Aleppo has since proven permanent and I believe it could be replicated on a smaller scale in Idlib territory positioned along Turkey's border. With U.S. assistance and a resumption of military support to U.S. vetted opposition groups active in the area, we have an opportunity to create a reality on the ground that is both safe and moderate. This would be an ink spot strategy with risks, but the potential benefits could be significant. This too would set into motion a chain of events that would likely lead to Al-Qaeda further isolating itself, as it acted in ways to protect its base. Only then would the United States have a clearer idea of who the genuinely committed transnational jihadists were, and where to target them.

Counter-Terrorism: Shia militants

Finally, the United States must also more clearly acknowledge the presence of other, non-Sunni terrorist organizations in Syria, and to work more determinedly to constrain their freedom of operation. Hezbollah is the most notable terrorist group in this case, but there are others too. Throughout the last administration's diplomatic attempts alongside Russia to introduce cessations of hostilities in Syria, Hezbollah and other designated organizations like Kataib Hezbollah were treated as legitimate actors, while Al-Qaeda and ISIS were excluded. Beyond the issue of the PKK, this inconsistency in policy weakens our hand enormously.

Enforced Zones of Calm

There is no perceivable opening for a grand, nationwide settlement to the conflict in Syria. As such, the best available interim solution is to introduce calm to geographically distinct zones in Syria, in which local Syrian actors and external actors with influence in the area can agree to freeze existing lines of conflict. This would be pursued alongside the above detailed counter-terrorism actions and would mean aiming to establish, and most importantly, to *enforce*, multiple zones of calm across Syria, in which conflict effectively ends, frontlines are frozen, and minimal reconstruction can begin.

In today's dynamics, five such zones come to mind: (1) the existing zone under Turkish influence in northern Aleppo; (2) a new zone under Turkish influence in northern Idlib; (3) the formalization of a zone of stability under SDF influence in northeastern Syria; (4) a new zone of stability in southern and southwestern Syria, under the influence of Jordan and Israel; and (5) a new, future zone of stability in eastern Syria, divided between the Assad regime and newly formed, local U.S.-backed anti-ISIS forces.

Creating these zones of calm along Syria's borders will assist in an eventual managed process of refugee resettlement, easing the burden placed on Syria's neighbors. It would also help slow or even stop the flow of weapons and money intended for armed activities from flowing across these border areas, while the stability itself will give opposition territories the opportunity to demonstrate their latent capabilities in local governance and service provision. Until now, those latent capabilities have been sharply limited by sustained aerial bombing, a challenge that neither the Assad regime nor the YPG have faced.

Creating multiple facts on the ground in this case would make it impossible for Bashar al-Assad to credibly claim an intent to recapture every inch of his territory. It would in and of itself represent a considerable source of pressure on Assad's claim of unending leadership in Syria and may eventually allow for conditions in which a determined move by the international community to initiate meaningful negotiations could actually make progress. For this reason, the United States would need to pursue an intensive track of bilateral negotiations with Russia throughout the lead-up to, and during the formative stage of these zones of stability. That dialogue would be exclusively focused on determining a shared understanding of what kind of political future in Syria was acceptable to both parties.

These zones of calm would face multiple determined spoilers, particularly Assad himself. This is why the United States and allied countries must be prepared to enforce these zones of stability through a credible threat of punitive action for violators. Al-Qaeda, ISIS and other militant actors would pose similarly significant spoiling threats, and should face similar punitive actions.

Regarding the enforcement aspect specifically, the threat of force can create meaningful diplomatic leverage, but only when it is credible and part of a clearly defined strategy. The recent cruise missile strikes on Syria did have an effect on the behavior of certain states, but the lack of a strategic foundation meant that our adversaries have now returned to business as usual. While it is indeed important, even necessary, to enforce established international norms such as that that forbids the use of chemical weapons, it is also important to establish moral equivalency and to recognize that other conventional means of killing are often far more effective and used with impunity. For example, monitoring data suggests that chemical weapons have been responsible for under 1% of all civilian casualties in Syria, while the Assad regime's use of air-dropped bombs has been responsible for 57% of all civilian fatalities. It should not be a matter of the murder weapon that defines whether murder is acceptable or not.

Pursuing this 'zones of stability' strategy would be far from easy and success may seem hard to come by at first. But treating Syria as a multitude of different mini conflict zones makes more sense than treating it as one whole. Moreover, the power of calm and the threat of serious consequences for violating that calm has a good chance of eventually establishing a deterrence dynamic. The additional pressure that it would place upon terrorist groups and on Assad himself, should provide the United States with more options and more leverage than exist today.

Iran

The United States must urgently acknowledge and act to confront the malign activities of Iran in exploiting pre-existing instability in the Middle East to undermine its rivals and to establish hegemonic influence for itself. While constructive relations with Iran are arguably in the interest of all members of the international community, the revolutionary nature of its regional policy and its impressive success in utilizing unconventional means to assert strong levels of influence against the United States represents a sustained threat to the United States' position of influence in the Middle East. It also represents a serious threat to Israel. Increased Iranian confidence in Syria has recently transitioned into increasingly bold threats against Israel – from the creation of Shia militia groups with the proclaimed objective of liberating territory controlled by Israel, stationing Shia militants in Syria near Israeli territory with anti-aircraft weapons, or in providing further strategic weaponry to Hezbollah.

The United States' best method of pressure on Iran and its use of militant groups in Syria is the use of targeted sanctions, especially against airlines used to fly weaponry and militiamen daily from Iran to Damascus. The United States may also choose to further strengthen economic sanctions and other measures against Hezbollah and to seek some extent of an understanding with Russia, in order to test the theory that Russia may diverge from Iran in terms of their respective visions for Syria's future.

Chairman ROYCE. Thank you.
Dr. Dafna Rand.

STATEMENT OF DAFNA H. RAND, PH.D., ADJUNCT PROFESSOR, NATIONAL DEFENSE UNIVERSITY

Ms. RAND. Thank you. Thank you. Good morning, Chairman Royce, Ranking Member Engel, members of the committee. Thank you for inviting me to testify.

Mr. Chairman, you mentioned the White Helmets and I would like to start there because I agree that it is a remarkable story. I would note that 140 or so of these White Helmets, these civilian protection forces, have been directly targeted when they go out to rescue. So there have been 140 casualties in the past 2 years alone. That is just one statistic of the suffering, displacement, and state-led atrocities that have occurred in Syria. Eighty percent of the population is now in need of humanitarian assistance, 12 million Syrians are displaced inside and outside the country. In short, this is the greatest humanitarian tragedy and crisis in our current world today.

So thank you, Mr. Chairman and Ranking Member Engel, and members of the committee for making and keep the Syrian people at the center of your policymaking work here.

The strikes on April 6th may have been a justifiable appropriate response to the use of sarin gas against Khan Sheikhoun. Yet, these strikes appear to be divorced from a larger strategy for U.S. engagement. It is particularly alarming that the administration comments on Syria policy after these strikes continue to be so disjointed and unclear. Americans, our allies, and the Syrian people would benefit from understanding what these strikes signify and where they fit within the larger policy goals.

I see at least four objectives for the U.S. in Syria and each will require a sustained strategy that combines public and private diplomacy. None of these will succeed without a fully staffed and empowered State Department serving as a coequal in the interagency and none of them can be sustained without adequate foreign assistance.

First, as my colleagues have mentioned, a negotiated agreement in the de-escalation of the fighting should be the most immediate and most important objective. Fighting ISIS, countering WMD, helping civilians, these goals are very critical but they will all be enabled by conflict resolution. Because this is a foundational objective, it is alarming to read public statements from the administration flippantly suggesting that whether Assad stays or goes is irrelevant. Defining the end game as a negotiated settlement between the regime and the opposition is the critical first task.

Secretary Tillerson will have to use these strikes and the leverage they have generated to push Moscow back to a position where it will be able and willing to be a genuine partner. That means holding Moscow accountable publicly and privately when ceasefires promised by the regime never materialize and when aid convoys promised by Damascus and organized by the U.N. never reach the besieged areas.

It is true that pushing Moscow and Tehran to make Damascus concede will be very, very tough but we have leverage. For example, let's refuse CT cooperation to Moscow if it doesn't comply with the next round of de-escalation or humanitarian talks.

Second, defeating ISIS is an obvious priority but the administration needs to be smart about the diplomacy and foreign assistance that will sustain any military offensive. Pushing Daesh out of Raqqa will be the easy part. What will be hard will be working with Turkey to negotiate YPG influence, as has been mentioned, or to ensure that the SAC, the Syrian Arab Coalition, and the SDF, the combination of Kurdish and Arab liberators, can effectively govern this very vast area of Syria.

What we know about global terrorism is this: They prey on ungoverned spaces remote from central control, where citizens are disaffected and angry. We cannot let these territories of Syria fall into this trap again. And that is why I am particularly concerned about rumored and alleged reductions in things like food aid or reductions in support for governance to local councils that will be formed in the wake of the Daesh liberation in these areas of Syria.

And because a sustainable defeat of ISIS requires regional consideration, I am concerned about reports that ESF to Jordan, to Tunisia, to Lebanon are reportedly going to be cut.

Third, the chemical weapons deterrence is a key objective. The strikes may deter Assad from using CW again. We don't really know because he has been using CW as a weapon of desperation. Still, we need to also continue the really hard multilateral diplomatic work.

I would note Russia's relative cooperation with the 2013 U.N. Resolutions on the U.N. regarding Syria's gas attack and what generally the 2013 to 2014 U.N. Organization for the Prohibition of Chemical Weapons, the OPCW's efforts to destroy 1300 tons of weapons. Clearly, this was imperfect. Clearly, there was cheating and hidden weapons but for Syria's neighbors and for the citizens and for U.S. troops on the ground, certainly destroying something was better than nothing. And that is why today multilateral diplomacy is critical. That is why we need to continue to support the OPCW and U.N. investigatory bodies and we will need to do this through diplomacy by pushing the Russians and other members of the international community.

Fourth, protecting the Syrian people must remain at the heart of U.S. policy in Syria. This effort includes humanitarian assistance, support for civil society, and support for local governance in liberated and opposition-controlled areas, and it includes accountability measure for the ongoing human rights violations and atrocities that have been committed, including accountability for the Khan Sheikhoun attack.

Since the start of this conflict, the U.S. has been the largest single bilateral donor of humanitarian assistance to the Syrian people but in the past months, the aid that is flowing from the U.S. and other donor nations has not been reaching most of the Syrians in need. Some organizations on the ground are estimating that only 10 percent of international aid is arriving into opposition-controlled areas of Syria. That is over five million people. So this crisis of access will require continued American leadership.

In conclusion, absent a clear and consistent articulation of U.S. strategy toward Syria, these limited strikes earlier this month will have little to no material impact. In fact, there is a danger that our friends may feel, over time, even more betrayed, as many within Syria and the region cheered the strikes on the premise that they signaled a significant shift in policy.

A clear strategy will help us mobilize our partners. For example, at this particular moment, we need our Gulf partners to help us play a moderating role with the armed opposition. So pushing for the resumption of negotiations will be hard but a strategy that focuses on diplomacy and U.S. leadership is the only option.

Finally, I thank this committee for understanding how a fully funded, empowered State Department and U.S. Agency for International Development will be critical to pursue all of the objectives that I have outlined.

I look forward to your questions.

[The prepared statement of Ms. Rand follows:]

Syria After the Missile Strikes: Policy Options
Testimony before the House Committee on Foreign Affairs
Dr. Dafna H. Rand
National Defense University
April 27, 2017

Chairman Royce, Ranking Member Engel, Committee members, thank you for inviting me to testify today on an issue with direct implications for American values, interests, and global leadership. Six years after the Syria crisis began, it has become the twenty-first century's most severe humanitarian tragedy and one of its thorniest international security dilemmas. Nearly 500,000 Syrians have been killed, with the Bashar al-Assad regime directly responsible for the majority of these deaths. The displacement of 12 million Syrians has created a refugee crisis, challenging many of Syria's generous neighbors who are struggling to absorb those fleeing for their lives. In perpetuating the conflict, Assad and his Russian and Iranian allies have undermined the U.S.-led international liberal order, including global norms regarding the protection of civilians during conflict.

The April 6 U.S. missile strikes on the Al Shayrat air base were an arguably justified response to the Syrian regime's unconscionable sarin gas attack on Khan Sheikhoun days earlier, but they appear to be entirely divorced from any strategy for U.S. engagement to resolve the Syrian crisis. For targeted strikes such as these to have an impact on the overall arc of the conflict, they cannot be launched in a vacuum. They must represent one aspect of a broader diplomatic strategy utilizing economic, political, and other security levers.

Any short-term benefits conferred by the strikes will erode, absent a multi-prolonged diplomatic strategy. Syrian civilians who cheered the strikes will see them as a momentary engagement by an Administration that otherwise has shown little interest in addressing Syrian suffering. In the aftermath of these strikes, the Administration must identify key policy objectives and design strategies to achieve them. These objectives include: a negotiated agreement to de-escalate the fighting; defeating ISIS in Syria in a way that is sustainable; continued counter-proliferation efforts to stop the Assad regime from using chemical weapons; and renewed efforts to protect Syrian civilians and to deliver lifesaving humanitarian aid. To achieve these policies will require a fully funded State Department; diplomats and civilian aid experts will be responsible for a strategy that combines non-military coercion with public and private diplomacy.

Ending the Syrian Civil War, through a Transition to a New Governing Body

Three weeks after the Al Shayrat air base attacks, it is still unclear whether U.S. policy toward the Syrian regime and the Syrian civil conflict has shifted. As a candidate, President Trump espoused an isolationist approach, even specifically warning in 2013 against military intervention in Syria.[1] Indeed, during the week before the strikes, the Administration publicly rolled out what appeared to be a coordinated, significant policy shift, with multiple public statements by both Secretary Tillerson and Ambassador Haley that a transition away from Assad was no longer a U.S. policy priority.[2] These statements likely encouraged Assad to use chemical weapons in Khan Sheikhoun. Yet in the wake of the Al Shayrat strikes, these same Cabinet members and other senior Administration officials reversed course and issued public statements remarkably consistent with those issued by the Obama administration, making it clear that Assad's departure would be necessary to end the Syrian civil war.[3]

It is urgent that the White House clarify U.S. policy and stand behind the need for Assad to step down, in line with the 2012 Geneva Communiqué. This document called for the establishment of a transitional governing body with full executive powers, to include members of the Syrian government and opposition. This Communiqué was endorsed by the UN Security Council – including Russia – and endures as the most practical basis for an eventual negotiated political settlement. Any movement away from this policy would embolden Assad and his backers, including Iran and Hezbollah. This not only would perpetuate the Syrian conflict and endanger countless more Syrian civilians; it also would expand the grave threat posed by Hezbollah to Syria's neighbors, particularly Israel.

In pushing for a negotiated end to the civil war, the Administration should seek to leverage the Al Shayrat strikes to help further multilateral and unilateral diplomatic efforts. Coercive diplomacy must be used to push Russia to resume negotiations on military de-escalation (i.e. meaningful ceasefires) and humanitarian access. Despite many efforts, both tracks failed in 2016 because Russia believed it had the upper hand and was unwilling or incapable of pushing its proxy in Damascus to comply. Hopefully, Secretary Tillerson used his recent trip to Moscow to make clear that continued Russian support for Assad will be met with additional U.S. sanctions on Russian entities. (And to use whatever threat of further military force may indeed worry Moscow.) The strikes also offer an opportunity to warn Iran regarding its support for the regime in Damascus, and to push both Russia and Iran to make commitments to rein in Damascus ahead of the next Astana meeting that they are hosting in early May.

There are other tools available in the Administration's tool kit to accelerate pressure against Damascus, including the new sanctions authorities offered in the *Caesar Syrian Civilian*

---

[1] Nicholas Fandos, "Trump's View of Syria: How it Evolved in 19 Tweets," *The New York Times,* April 7, 2017, https://www.nytimes.com/2017/04/07/us/politics/donald-trump-syria-twitter.html?_r=0

[2] Elise Labbot, Nicole Gaouette, and Richard Roth, "US Signals Openness to Assad Staying Put," *CNN Politics,* March 30, 2017, http://www.cnn.com/2017/03/30/politics/tillerson-haley-syria-assad-turkey/index.html.

[3] Angela Dewan, "U.S. Envoy Nikki Haley Says Syrian Regime Change is Inevitable," *CNN Politics,* April 10, 2017, http://www.cnn.com/2017/04/09/middleeast/syria-missile-strike-chemical-attack-aftermath/index.html.

Protection Act. However, leveraging the strikes into a comprehensive pressure strategy must be done quickly, because whatever new momentum offered by the strikes will dissipate.

Defeating the ISIS Caliphate in Syria

Since January, the Trump Administration has talked repeatedly about increasing its efforts to defeat ISIS, but it remains unclear how the strategy for countering ISIS relates to the Administration's overall Syria policy goals. In less than three months, the While House has nearly doubled the number of ground troops in Syria to support U.S. partners engaged in the ISIS fight.[4] A liberation offensive to rout ISIS from Raqqa is imminent.[5] Yet while the policy goal of eliminating ISIS' safe haven and command center in Syria is clear, the strategic conundrums inherent in this proposition remain unresolved.

First, the Administration has not explained to the American people why it is increasing U.S. boots on the ground in Syria. Americans deserve to know the extent to which ground forces will participate in the dangerous fight against ISIS in Syria's northern and eastern regions and for how long U.S. forces will remain in Syria training their partners.

Second, the post-conflict stabilization strategy remains murky: Will the Kurdish YPG (the People's Protection Units) and other Syrian Democratic Forces who represent the key ground forces in the liberation operation govern this mostly Arab territory? Has this plan been pre-coordinated with Turkey? Will the YPG and other Kurdish forces tacitly cooperate with the Assad regime, once ISIS has been defeated, thus complicating U.S. policy even further? How will the United States ensure that the YPG liberators will protect the rights of the local Syrian population, thereby preventing another cycle of grievance that could yield yet another generation of future terrorists? Planning for the actual Raqqa operation is relatively straightforward, but figuring out what to do when the U.S.-backed forces succeed is not.

Neighbors such as Turkey are keenly interested in the question of who will rule large swaths of Syrian territory in ISIS' wake, particularly if the YPG fighting force prevails. The planning for the post-liberation stabilization period in Syria is a significant diplomatic effort. It will have to be carefully integrated into the overall policy planning for the resumption of diplomacy between the regime and the opposition discussed above.

---

[4] In March, President Trump deployed 400 more troops to Syria, bringing the number of ground troops to 1,000. See Lucas Tomlinson, *"Turkish Jets Bomb U.S.-backed Forces,"* Fox News World, April 25, 2017, http://www.foxnews.com/world/2017/04/25/turkish-jets-bomb-us-backed-forces-in-iraq-syria-us-officials-say.html.

[5] Aaron Stein, "Raqqa: A Very Long and Nasty Fight," *The Cipher Brief,* March 17, 2017, https://www.thecipherbrief.com/article/middle-east/very-long-and-nasty-fight-1089.

Reports that the Administration plans to cut Fiscal Year 2018 regional stabilization funds and economic support funds to neighbors such as Jordan are deeply problematic, as these types of cuts will undermine the sustainability of any near-term win against ISIS. Within Syria itself, cutting humanitarian and governance assistance to the people liberated from ISIS will be self-defeating. International assistance is necessary to ensure that those who once lived under ISIS rule are now offered basic services and humanitarian assistance. This type of assistance represents a relatively modest investment with a potentially significant return – sustainable stabilization can protect these territories from ever again becoming a safe haven for radical terrorist groups.

Preventing the Proliferation of Chemical Weapons

Explaining the strikes on April 6, President Trump referred directly to a counter-proliferation policy goal, saying: "It is in this vital national security interest of the United States to prevent and deter the spread and use of deadly chemical weapons." Secretary Mattis' public remarks since the Al Shayrat strikes suggest that, at least from a Department of Defense perspective, preventing the use of chemical weapons (CW) was the key policy objective of the strikes.[6] In a public statement issued this week while visiting Israel, Secretary Mattis again warned Assad against using chemical weapons.[7]

Yet if the urgent policy goal from the U.S. military's perspective is to prevent the Syrian regime from using sarin gas and other CW in the future, the deterrent effect of the limited strikes may prove to be insufficient. Deterrence should be accompanied by the physical destruction of chemical weapons caches – an effort requiring difficult multilateral diplomacy. While the agreement had many flaws, overall the 2013 U.S.-Russian mechanism to work with the United Nations and the Organization for the Prohibition of Chemical Weapons (OPCW) to destroy Syria's declared CW stockpiles severely limited Assad's ability to use these weapons against U.S. troops, allies such as Israel, or Syrian civilians. Assad's illegal secret retention of CW stocks or capacity to regenerate them violated international law, but the CW threat to Syrian civilians and to the United States and our allies would have been far worse in the absence of the 2013 agreement. On balance, OPCW's post-2013 presence in Syria, with Russian support, has advanced U.S. counter-proliferation goals, making it harder for the Syrian regime to use these horrific weapons.

---

[6] Secretary Mattis told reporters that "the purpose of this attack was singularly against chemical weapons use," on April 11, 2017. Ryan Browne, "Mattis on Syria: ISIS Remains the Priority but Chemical Weapons Will Not Be Tolerated," *CNN Politics*, April 11, 2017, http://www.cnn.com/2017/04/11/politics/mattis-syria-isis-chemical/index.html.

[7] "Defense Secretary Mattis Warns Syria Still has Chemical Weapons," *CBS NEWS*, April 21, 2017, http://www.cbsnews.com/news/defense-secretary-james-mattis-warns-syria-still-has-chemical-weapons/

In addition to continuing to use further strikes should Assad again use CW, a new round of multilateral diplomacy will be necessary to protect earlier counter-proliferation efforts. Last week, the Russians vetoed a UN Security Council Resolution calling for an investigation into the Khan Sheikhoun attacks. Russia's intransigence and disinformation campaign on the Khan Sheikhoun attacks contrasts starkly with its relatively cooperative approach in 2013. This regression is worrisome.

Russia may be at odds with the United States in terms of its overall policy goals in Syria, but we need Russian cooperation and support on limited issues such as counter-proliferation. Strong, multilateral diplomacy will be required to push Russia toward, at a minimum, returning to the moderate levels of cooperation on CW issues that occurred from 2013-2017.

Finally, as part of the effort to deter Assad from any further CW use, the U.S. must lead multilateral efforts to maintain the international opprobrium focused on Syria in the wake of the Khan Sheikhoun attacks. The Administration should coordinate with European allies and other partners to set the record straight in the face of Russian disinformation campaigns, continuing to declassify and make public U.S. information that demonstrates the Assad regime's culpability for this gruesome use of sarin gas against Syrian civilians. It should press European and other partners to do the same.

Protecting Syrian Civilians, Providing Humanitarian Relief, and Promoting Accountability

Protecting the Syrian people must remain at the heart of U.S. policy in Syria. This effort includes humanitarian assistance; support for civil society in liberated, opposition-controlled areas; and accountability for ongoing human rights violations, including the Khan Sheikhoun attack. Since the start of the conflict, the United States has been the largest single bilateral donor of humanitarian assistance to the Syrian people. In the past months, however, the aid flowing from the United States and other donors has not been reaching most of the Syrians in need. Some organizations on the ground are estimating that only 10 percent of international aid is arriving into opposition-controlled areas of Syria (where over 5 million Syrians reside), because the Assad regime is deliberately holding up cross-border aid in violation of UN Security Council Resolution 2254.

The Administration has yet to explain how the Al Shayrat strikes fit into any strategy to ensure civilian protection, or how the United States will respond to other equally horrific, non-CW attacks against Syrian civilians. Almost immediately after the U.S. strikes, the Syrian regime used Al Shayrat as the base for additional bombing campaigns against Syrian civilians. The Syrian Air Force has already resumed aerial bombings of Khan Sheikhoun using conventional weapons.[8] There are a number of levers available to the U.S. government to deter and punish Syrian officials – and their Russian and Iranian champions – who are involved in deliberately targeting civilians. The Trump Administration should focus on sanctioning individual perpetrators, as authorized in the *Caesar Syrian Civilian Protection Act.*

Finally, even though immediate justice for these crimes sadly is improbable, the Administration has opportunities to maintain U.S. leadership on longer-term accountability efforts by the international community. Ensuring appropriate documentation of these human rights violations is vital. The United States has been a leading donor in the arena of international accountability efforts in the past, and opportunities exist to demonstrate that U.S. statements on accountability for Khan Sheikhoun and other violations of international law are more than just empty words. Continued U.S. leadership at the United Nations will ensure that the highly effective UN Commission of Inquiry on Syria can continue its work to gather evidence and to document violations.

Conclusion: The Risks of Foregoing a Mature Strategy in Favor of Inchoate Tactics

Absent a clear and consistent articulation of U.S. strategy toward Syria, the limited strikes earlier this month will have little to no material impact. Many of our allies cheered on these strikes, yet these friends may have done so assuming a major U.S. strategic shift toward greater military intervention where none exists. An articulation of a strategy will also help our allies contribute to the diplomatic efforts that should follow the strikes – such as pushing Gulf partners to deliver some of the armed opposition groups to the Astana talks in May or urging European partners to join the United States in sanctioning Russian, Iranian, and Syrian military officials who have perpetrated crimes against the Syrian people.

The April 6 strikes only offer leverage if they can jump-start a new strategy combining economic sanctions, multilateral counter-proliferation efforts, and new investments in diplomatic negotiations. Following the strikes, U.S. diplomats must push the regime and its Russian and Iranian backers toward a de-escalation plan that may allow for opposition-regime talks. European allies should offer their own set of new sanctions against Syrian, Iranian, and Russian officials. Driving ISIS out of Syria will require a careful assistance plan to support local governance and humanitarian assistance for the mostly Arab Syrians who have been living under ISIS rule. None of these strategies can be executed without a fully funded, empowered State Department and U.S. Agency for International Development – mobilized to advance U.S. leadership and influence in pursuit of these objectives.

---

[8] Louisa Loveluck and Zakaria Zakaria, "Despite U.S. Missile Barrage Syria Continues Airstrikes Against Rebels," *The Washington Post*, April 8, 2017, https://www.washingtonpost.com/world/warplanes-return-to-syrian-town-devastated-by-chemical-attack/2017/04/08/38a5d8cc-1bdc-11e7-8598-9a99da559f9e_story.html.

Chairman ROYCE. Thank you.

You know it seems that Russia and Iran have very different goals here for Syria and some of you have commented on that. In terms of trying to figure out next steps, it looks as through the goal on the part of the Iranians is a land bridge that would stretch to Hezbollah-controlled southern Lebanon, where for some time now the Islamic Republic of Iran has been trying to move these larger and larger missiles or longer range missiles. I guess this morning there are reports that the IDF put a strike in against a shipment that had landed of these missiles, right?

So, as Iran's obsession with their stated policy of wiping Israel off the map continues, you have Moscow with a very different goal. Their goal is not to wipe out Israel. Their goal seems to be to increase Russia's leverage. And I wonder if that suggests that the two could be split here in terms of the long-term interest of trying to get some stability, because as long as the Iranians remain on the ground, the problem there is going to be the recruitment of training for additional Hezbollah units that you are now seeing, as well as the in-migration of the Revolutionary Guard Corps on the ground, and these other entities, they are not seeking to calm the situation. I mean all across the Middle East they are creating additional, whether it is Yemen or Bahrain, they are involved in conflict.

And I would just ask our panelists for their opinion on a strategy that would allow some kind of a direct negotiation on that concept and whether you think it would be possible because that might allow us then to move Assad out of the equation and bring in someone else on the Alawite side that would have an interest in the long-term survivability of Syria as a state.

Mr. Singh.

Mr. SINGH. Sure. Well, Mr. Chairman, I think you are absolutely right about differing Russian and Iranian interests, as I mentioned in my testimony.

I think the challenge is in the short-term I think there is a sort of co-dependency between Russia, and Iran, and Syria. They need each other. Russia is providing actually quite a small military force but a decisive one, providing air cover, for example, for the ground forces which are largely provided by the Iranians. The Iranians have contributed, from the numbers I have seen, upwards of 100,000 fighters, not Iranians all but Iranian-backed fighters. So theirs is sort of complementary to Russian and Iranian activities there and I think either would be hard-pressed to succeed without the other.

But I do think that Iran is committed to the Assad regime in a way that, perhaps over the long-run, Russia isn't because I think that Iran could not be guaranteed its position in Syria with any ruler other than Bashar al-Assad, even if it were someone else from his sector, someone else from his sort of territory.

And it does, over the long-run, perhaps open up the possibility of splitting the two. But I think it is very much over the long-run. I think it is not something that it is there in the short-term.

Perhaps the Russians will come to see that they are embroiled in a counterinsurgency that there is very little easy escape from. No one is going to come and rescue the Russians from the insurgency which they are facing around Idlib, and Aleppo, and so on and so forth. We are certainly not going to. We certainly shouldn't and I don't think anyone else is prepared to do so either. And hope-fully, that will prompt the Russians, at some point, to recognize, especially if there is a credible threat of American military force.

Chairman ROYCE. Well, maybe Mr. Lister can comment on this but it seems to me that the Russian objective here is partly to maintain access to the Mediterranean. Their goal is not necessarily to see this thing deepen and yet, for the Iranians, they are gaining battlefield experience for their forces. They are honing their skills. They are replacing Sunni populations with Lebanese Hezbollah families that they are bringing in to Old Damascus and areas like this. This is the exact opposite, it would seem to me, of Russia's long-term interest.

And so Mr. Lister, what is your observations?

Mr. LISTER. Thank you for the question.

For me, this is essentially about differing goals and differing needs between Iran and Russia. These are two countries playing extremely different, though as my colleague says, complementary roles in Syria.

For Russia, the objective is to compete and outplay the United States and to show that we aren't the power that we think we are, that we are not capable of exerting the kind of influence in the re-gion that we used to, and also, of course, immediately to shore up what was in 2011 Russia's most reliable and most intensive rela-tionship in the region, which was the Assad regime. Since the So-viet Union times, Russia has relied on the Syrian Army——

Chairman ROYCE. Right.

Mr. LISTER [continuing]. Intensively for a relationship in the re-gion, almost exclusively. And so for Russia, this is a strategic or geostrategic calculus, largely as a reflection of its rivalry with the United States.

And for Iran, this is a zero-sum issue. There is, as of now, in to-day's dynamics, no negotiation for Iran. It is Assad, or nothing, or we carry on fighting.

And the key issue, the key worry we should all have in our minds, is that we have invested so much energy over the last 2 or 3 years based on an assumption that Russia has the leverage nec-essary to result in the kind of policy result that we want, which is a negotiation process that means something and that results in a conclusion that we all want, which is an end to conflict and some extent of political transition in Damascus.

Unfortunately, as my colleague said, Russia is actually operating in Syria on a shoe string with very little ground influence, beyond Special Forces dotted around in a few specific areas.

You know I have spent the last 18 months meeting periodically with Russian officials who work on the Syrian issue. And one of the things they revealed to me, which is very interesting, is that as of 2 or 3 months ago, the assessment within Moscow was that the Syrian Army had no more than 20,000 offensively deployable, suffi-ciently trained, and loyal soldiers that the Russian Government was willing to work alongside—20,000 for all of Syria. It is a pit-tance.

In comparison, the Iranian Government has successfully estab-lished what I would estimate to be at least 150,000 militiamen,

Syrians, predominately, but also Iraqis, Lebanese, Syrians, Afghans, Pakistanis, and possibly some Yemenis. Twenty thousand Syrian forces as compared to 150,000 militiamen who are there potentially to die for a religious cause, rather than for a strategic cause, is an issue we need to worry about in terms of how we invest our resources, in terms of pushing things to create the possible conditions for the result that we want.

Chairman ROYCE. Thank you. Mr. Engel.

Mr. ENGEL. Thank you, Mr. Chairman. Before I ask my questions, I ask unanimous consent to enter two statements into the record. One is a statement by Raed al-Saleh, head of the Syria Civil Defense, as you mentioned before, known as the White Helmets, on behalf of Nobel Peace Prize-nominated rescue organization that has rescued over 90,000 Syrian lives.

Chairman ROYCE. Without objection.

Mr. ENGEL. And the second statement is from Church World Service.

Chairman ROYCE. Again, without objection.

Mr. ENGEL. Thank you, Mr. Chairman.

The White House Press Secretary Sean Spicer said in a press briefing, shortly after the U.S. airstrikes, if you gas a baby, if you put a barrel bomb into innocent people, I think you will see a response from this President.

This appeared to add a new red line to U.S. policy that Assad's use of barrel bombs, an all too frequent occurrence, would invite a U.S. response. But later the White House clarified that he meant chlorine-filled barrel bombs.

Now for anyone who thinks that I am going tough on the White House, maybe you should know that I was equally tough on the previous administration's miscalculation that Assad would somehow fall and so cause them to do things or not do things. And of course, here we are many years later, Assad hasn't fallen. I think we made a terrible mistake when we didn't aid the Free Syrian Army 4 years ago, when the President's national security team all was in favor. I think it was a miscalculation. I also think when you draw lines in the sand, you need to back up those lines but you also need to be consistent.

And what we are seeing from the administration is there is an introduction and retraction of new red lines. It muddies U.S. strategy in Syria. And as I mentioned before, I think it is very important that the President tell the Congress what his plans are in Syria and then the Congress needs to give him authorization to make any kind of military moves.

So when we have introduction and retraction of new red lines, it muddies the strategy in Syria. I want to ask Dr. Rand, how do we expect our allies and adversaries to react to this?

Ms. RAND. Thank you, Congressman Engel. This is a big concern of mine as well, that the inconsistency is sending different signals and that our allies will see in the administration and White House's different statements what they want to hear. Right? So certain allies have different views and they will seize on one Secretary or another Secretary's statements, if they diverge, to say that is U.S. administration policy. That is a concern.

On the issue of what is the red line, is it just a CW deterrence or is it a general deterrence about crimes against humanity, I would note that in the couple days after the sarin gas attacks, there were very damaging atrocities committed by the Syrian regime again. So if that, indeed, was Mr. Spicer's red line, it was passed already, shortly after the time he was making those statements.

But I would agree with the concern about allies. I would also add the concern about the Syrian people, who are left confused about what is the new shift in U.S. policy toward intervention.

Mr. ENGEL. Anybody else care to comment?

Mr. SINGH. Well, Congressman, I would agree with the general principle that credibility is important. And I think to have credibility, we also need to have clarity. I agree with that. And that is why it is important that we have a very rigorous policy process where we decide what are those lines are for the United States that sort of both threaten our interest, threaten civilians on the ground. What are we prepared to do in response? And then that we communicate those things to the appropriate channels. Sometimes a public message is right. Sometimes private messages to places like Moscow and elsewhere are the right methods.

But that all requires a rigorous policy process and I think that will be the key for us.

Mr. ENGEL. Thank you. Let me ask a question about the chemical weapons program. In 2013, the Organization for the Prohibition of Chemical Weapons certified, and we remember this, that it had removed 1300 tons of declared chemical weapons from Syria. And of course, we now know that Syria held back some chemical agents from declaration and removal because it used those agents in the April 4th sarin gas attack.

Now, I supported the U.S. response, as I said before, 59 Tomahawk missiles, because I thought it was an appropriate demonstration to Syria and their Russian enablers that there would be consequences for the use of chemical weapons. But these strikes are not a long-term solution and they will not help to eliminate the threat posed by Syria's continued possession of chemical weapons. So let me ask any of the witnesses what recommendations do you have to work toward full implementation of the U.N. Security Council Resolution 2118, which sought to remove Syria's chemical weapons, and what particular responsibility does Moscow have in the implementation of this resolution and in removing chemical weapons from Syria?

Anyone who cares to answer.

Ms. RAND. Sure, I will start. I think this is an excellent point. And I mentioned in my testimony there is a JIM, the Joint Investigative Mechanism, that was commissioned by the U.N. in 2015 to go and actually name perpetrators and some of the chemical weapons. And this mandate was extended last year to 2017. It will run out I think sometime this summer or the fall.

So it is really critical. This is an urgent diplomatic—again, it is not a sufficient diplomatic solution to the chemical weapons bomb, but it is part of the solution and it is urgent that the U.S. show its leadership at the U.N. and push Moscow and other powers to agree to continue this mandate of the JIM.

Mr. LISTER. I would add, if I may, you know frankly speaking, Russia bears the weight of responsibility for the fact that this chemical weapons attack took place. And we shouldn't forget that Russia had troops and almost certainly aircraft up until a certain time at this air base from which the attack was launched.

We should all be asking the question, and I am sure we all are, did Russia in fact know that the Assad regime had retained some extent of its chemical weapons capabilities. And if it did, then we would be justified in, I think, putting and placing more pressure, whether through sanctions or other diplomatic means, on the Russian Government to force it to see, through a broader package of policies on Syria, the more holistic one that I described in my opening statement.

But in the end, Russia isn't going to achieve its ultimate objective in Syria which is stability. For Russia, Syria is still something to be negotiated over. And I think what the Russians are discovering, almost on a week-by-week basis now, is that having invested resources in Syria and in rescuing the Assad regime, achieving their ultimate long-term objective isn't happening and it is not going to happen for a long time. So I do think we have a responsibility to put more pressure on Russia.

And more broadly, I think the sanctions on I think 271 Syrians connected to the chemical weapons program is a good step. I noted that a number of that size suggests that we are not just targeting senior officials but we are also targeting people further down the ladder of seniority and I think that is wise. I think using what I would term escalatory sanctions—starting from the ground level and moving up—is an excellent way of putting more pressure and a sense of paranoia within the regime's military, intelligence, and otherwise the regime's apparatus, that we know what they are doing. We know who they are. We know everything about them and they will face consequences for being involved in these kind of criminal acts. And I think there is a lot that we can do to add to that pressure further.

Mr. SINGH. If I could just make a brief point, Congressman. I want to make sure that there is a clear understanding that this is not just a humanitarian issue for the United States because the CWC is a nonproliferation treaty. And if we allow that nonproliferation treaty to be breached, I think that has strategic ramifications for the United States for nonproliferation broadly. So we need to keep that frame of reference in mind as well.

Mr. ENGEL. Thank you.

Chairman ROYCE. Okay, we go to Ileana Ros-Lehtinen of Florida.

Ms. ROS-LEHTINEN. Thank you so much, Mr. Chairman.

And while Congress must be consulted before any long-term escalation of force in Syria, I supported the missile strikes that took place earlier this month and I hope that they serve as a warning that the United States will no longer tolerate Assad's chemical weapons attacks against the innocent civilians. The missile strikes proved our willingness to use force. That is a necessary ingredient whose absence doomed any previous chance of a negotiated outcome in Syria.

But I am still very concerned about the lack of a comprehensive strategy in Syria, a problem that has stretched across both administrations and our seeming insistence on treating the symptoms, rather than the disease. And as so many of us have said over the years, it is not possible to defeat ISIS while Assad remains in power, I fear that our narrow focus on short-term tactical successes will only exacerbate the problems that we are trying to solve.

So I wanted to ask you, Mr. Lister, can we hope to defeat ISIS while Assad remains in power? A lot of you spoke about what would happen if. And how does Assad's presence and tactics contribute to the growth and the narrative appeal of ISIS, as well as the al-Qaeda-linked and other jihadist groups in Syria?

And if Assad is not removed by countering Iran, by finding leverage with Russia, or otherwise, is it possible for this conflict and its associated costs to come to an end?

Mr. LISTER. Thank you very much for a really excellent question. And I think to answer it, we need to consider context as well, some historical background, but I will stay in the immediate term for now.

The reason why we have had success against ISIS or one of the reasons why we have had success with little other negative knock-on effects up until now, is because ISIS purposefully detached itself from the other dynamics of the Syrian conflict. With the exception of about a 6-month period of time, ISIS never sought to work with the opposition. It never sought to become part of the revolution against the Assad regime. It explicitly sought to establish an Islamic State with or without help and it would kill anyone who got in its way.

And for that reason, we have been able to attack ISIS in isolation from the rest of the conflict with relative success, up until now, but I think, as I hope is becoming clear, we are now seeing some of those disadvantageous knock-on effects becoming clear. For example, our NATO ally Turkey is effectively now at war with our local partner fighting ISIS, as of last night. And all of that is because, as you say, we didn't base all of this on a more holistic strategy. We didn't appreciate enough all of the broader dynamics. So, that is today.

In terms of Assad staying, I think the most important thing to bear in mind here is some history. In 2003, when the United States prepared to invade Iraq, as in fact American troops crossed on day one, the Grand Mufti then in Syria, the State-appointed, Assad-appointed Grand Mufti, issued a fatwa in which he declared it religiously obligatory on all Muslims globally to launch resistance movements in Iraq against American troops, using any means necessary. And that order was given to men and women. And that was, essentially, an instruction from the Assad Government.

Within 11 days of the U.S. invasion of Iraq, 5,000 foreign jihadi fighters crossed into Iraq, crossed Syria's borders; they flew into Aleppo and Damascus airports; were bussed in government buses to the Iraqi border and waived through open border crossings.

And in the 7 or 8 years that followed, during the war in Iraq, it would not be an exaggeration, I think to say, that hundreds of American troops would still be alive if the Assad regime had not continued its assistance to ISIS' predecessor movement, the Islamic State in Iraq. ISIS wouldn't be what it was today if those foreign jihadi fighters hadn't been given a free hand to train in Syria, to use Syrian Government medical facilities, and then to cross Syria's borders into Iraq.

And that support for jihadists didn't stop when American troops left Iraq in 2010. In 2011, whilst the Assad regime was arresting pro-democracy protesters, and women, and children, it was releasing jihadists from prison. Two of the seven founding members of the al-Qaeda affiliate in Syria were released from prison at the beginning of the protests. At least ten, as far as I am aware, of ISIS' most senior leaders in Syria were released from Assad prisons under an amnesty in 2011.

And since then, it is common knowledge that, at the very least, trade in gas, trade in other resources, has continued between the Assad regime. In fact, this very government here has sanctioned several Syrian officials for facilitating those trades.

So the argument is right. I know I am taking some time but the argument is right to say that while Assad stays in power, there is very little chance that that kind of facilitation of jihadists for Syrian goals, for Assad regime reasons, will not continue. And most importantly, the narrative for their very existence will continue to exist.

Ms. Ros-Lehtinen. Thank you very much, sir.

Thank you, Mr. Chairman.

Chairman Royce. Thank you.

Mr. Greg Meeks from New York.

Mr. Meeks. Thank you, Mr. Chairman. And I want to thank all three of the witnesses. I think you have been absolutely excellent and very insightful. And I really appreciate your testimony.

Let me start by stating declaratively I think that any rational, reasonable person would strongly, as I do, condemn the atrocities that took place in Syria and the utilization of chemical weapons but I believe just overall because, as one of the witnesses testified, people are dying, whether it is by chemical weapons or by conventional weapons. Death is death and they are dying by the numbers and we have to make sure we get a handle on that. And that we must, and the whole international community, must put our best efforts into addressing the crises there.

That has been what my position has been since the start of the conflict and it remains so today. That being said, many of my colleagues here, and as you have indicated, I think each and every one of you have indicated your thoughts on what should be next. I wish that the President of the United States would also tell us, as Members of Congress, what should be or what the strategy is next. You know we cannot be left wondering after the launch of 59 Tomahawk cruise missiles what Congress is to do. Congress should never be left wondering what next after the use of military force and never, especially in a situation where there is no imminent threat to our homeland. The United States needs—and why is that? Because we have a Constitution and the President should abide by that Constitution. And so the President should get congressional authorization for military action.

And as I sit here, I am extremely uneasy that we have no updated AUMF. And the President has stated, basically, that he has acted impulsively, without clearly articulating a strategy on Syria. Why do I know that? Because the President said he happened to have seen a picture of babies and that made him decide to do something that he had said just a few weeks before that he wasn't going to do. So he just acted impulsively, without a real strategy as to what to do next.

And when we talk about drawing red lines, and I felt this also, when President Obama had the red line, he came to Congress. Congress punted on what to do in Syria.

So I would hope as we look to and ask President Trump to come to Congress, and I hope he does, that we don't punt. We listen to the issues. Let's take the responsibility ourselves.

The most difficult decision for me, and I have been here for 19 years, the most difficult vote that I have had to make is the vote to make the determination of whether or not we were going to authorize the use of force, whether it was in the Kosovo struggles, in the Balkans when President Clinton was there, whether it was Iraq and Afghanistan. I want, and I think my constituents expect me, to have a vote in that regard and we must make sure that we have that. We cannot shirk our responsibility as Members of Congress.

And so I don't want to then say, whether it is President Trump or any other President after him, to say we punted, as Members of Congress, and then we criticized what the President did do or didn't do thereafter. Let us, I mean we should do our jobs.

Clearly, as I said, and someone mentioned Iraq, I think Mr. Lister did, clearly shock and awe. And many of us came back, many Members of Congress, came back after the shock and awe and we thought it was all over; we had won; it was victory. And then we saw that there was not strategy thereafter.

Let us have learned from that lesson that we can't just be so high and happy because we have had—there was a strike, 59 missiles that seemed to be sending a message that is over; we did the right thing. Let's talk now. Let's learn from what we didn't do in the past and talk a strategy and work with our allies.

I think that Dr. Rand talked about how important it is to make sure we are having a dialogue and a conversation with our allies as well as to make sure we are doing what is on the ground.

I think Mr. Lister was talking about how in fact during the war the Syrian Government was still active in putting folks in and trying to turn around the minds of individuals on the ground. Both he and Dr. Rand were absolutely correct. If we are cutting off humanitarian aid, if we are not putting in place things on the ground, if we are refusing to let refugees into the United States, we are not then doing what we need to do to make sure that even the folks on the ground to keep ISIS, or Daesh, as I call them, from recruit- ing individuals on the ground thinking that we are the bad guys. So I really had a question but I am out of time. I was just so impressed with your testimony and with the way that you have been answering questions.

You know I think, Mr. Chairman, maybe this is the youngest panel we have had. We need to make sure we have more young people whose future is really on the line. They are really thinking about tomorrow because it is their today. And so this is on both sides, all the witnesses, you and Mr. Engel should be really complimented about the witnesses that you have brought here today.

Chairman ROYCE. Thank you, Mr. Meeks.

We now go to Dana Rohrabacher of California.

Mr. ROHRABACHER. Thank you very much and I would like to echo what Mr. Meeks just said about the value of the testimony today.

What is interesting is you sort of dumped a heap of facts onto us and you are trying to make some sense out of it, like some sort of a jigsaw puzzle. And here you are. You have studied this, you have spent your whole time studying, and you can't come up with what the jigsaw maps out of this quagmire is. And so we appreciate you letting us know the series of facts that we need to deal with and maybe we can work together and come up with some ideas.

I was heartened that our chairman, Mr. Royce, whom I have deep respect for, during his questions mentioned how we might really benefit negotiating with Russia on this issue.

Chairman ROYCE. Well, I didn't get to the second part of my question. We would replace Putin, as well as Assad, in negotiations. I just wanted to clarify, Mr. Rohrabacher.

Mr. ROHRABACHER. But what we heard today is that there was a civil war in Syria, an organized effort supported by outsiders to overthrow the Government of Assad. That civil war, where people came in to support that has now morphed into regional anarchy, basically. And let me just say that I don't believe that Assad was any more brutal, any more dictatorial than a number of our friends and allies in that region. If there was a civil war being financed against any number of those governments, they would wipe out their opponents. And I do believe there is a moral equivalency between dropping a bomb on people and killing those same people with gas. You are killing innocent people. We have to stop the killing and we have seen that there is killing of innocent people.

And obviously, when we bombed, we ended up bombing their air base because 85 civilians suffered effects from gas and died. At the same time, while we are engaged in bombing in other parts nearby, and our bombs are killing ten times or five times that number of civilians, no. The killing should stop. That should be our goal and we should be willing to work with Russia in order to try to find some overall regional solution now and it shouldn't just be Assad has to go.

Let me just suggest what Erdogan is doing now, especially in his latest attacks, Erdogan is doing more damage to our national security by his basically power grab inside his own country and his Islamicization of his own country, he is doing much more damage than Assad could ever have dreamed of doing to our security. And yet, we are going to continue giving support to Mr. Erdogan, even after this incredible power grab that he has just participated in, a corrupt election that gives him the power to move that country. And now we find he is actually attacking Kurds now, rather than just trying to work with us in some ways.

Here is the question. All these facts that you are talking about and—again, I appreciate, deeply appreciate the facts that you have given us today to consider. Do we now need, if we are going to have peace in that region, a regional type of grand meeting somewhere like they did after World War I, and redraw the borders, and have newly accepted areas where the Kurds could have their area, and you could have various recognition, rather than trying to have a situation where today it obviously isn't working and we obviously have a double standard for Assad and Russia than we do for our own friends?

So let me put that out on the table.

Mr. SINGH. Thank you, Congressman. I think that the way I would interpret what has happened here in Syria is maybe a little bit different in the sense that I see in 2011 a peaceful protest that was brutally suppressed by the Assad regime.

Mr. ROHRABACHER. And do you think any of our allies, the Saudis, the Qataris, the Kuwaitis, if they thought that there was a civil war being financed by some other country in their region, would not have been just as brutal as Assad was?

Mr. SINGH. Well, sir, I don't think that that was what happened here. I think this was, actually, as I said, peaceful protests by Syrians that were suppressed by the Syrian regime. And I think that the Syrian regime created the conditions for the rise of an extremist opposition that, as Charles pointed out——

Mr. ROHRABACHER. But you are talking about an evolution because what happens is, we have seen it over and over again, peaceful demonstrations, you have a dictator, a gangster, he slaughters innocent people and then all of a sudden it escalates. That has happened a dozen times.

Mr. SINGH. Well this is on a very different scale, Congressman, than anything that has happened in the region, as I think Dr. Rand pointed out because you have hundreds of thousands of people, millions of people displaced. And I think what we really need is now to show leadership, which we didn't show in the past, to get on the same page of our allies to try to resolve the situation, where we haven't in the past.

Chairman ROYCE. Okay, we need to go to Mr. Bill Keating of Massachusetts.

Mr. KEATING. Well thank you, Mr. Chairman. And I want to thank the chairman and the ranking member because this committee, since I have been involved in it for several years now, has been thoughtful, and substantive in its action, and instrumental in many of our policies.

And along those lines, I want to just mention that as valuable as the testimony is today, I want to see going forward. I see a pattern on these issues where we are not having Trump administration officials in front of this committee and I think that is important to flesh out the strategy itself.

Chairman ROYCE. That is a good point, and if the gentleman will yield for a moment, Mr. Engel and I have had the opportunity to speak to the Secretary of State and we are extending an invitation to the committee.

Mr. KEATING. I am not surprised. Thank you, Mr. Chairman.

Chairman ROYCE. Thank you, Mr. Keating.

Mr. KEATING. And I just want to comment, too, that that will help flesh out a strategy and that is what we are talking about here.

You know today's testimony and the brutal conflict itself has proven that ending these atrocities and reaching a resolution requires a strategy, a strategy that reflects the complexities on the ground and cooperation at the international level. And I think a one-off military strike, which I thought was appropriate, yet one that wasn't followed up with a plan, and the inadequate staff in the State Department to meaningful engage, and also budget proposals that undermine our ability to be strategic are all issues.

Now, I also want to concentrate on something that I struggle with, and I think it has been brought up in today's testimony and that's the fact that Mr. Lister, in particular, started along these lines. In one sense, we are getting testimony and a general feeling among people looking at this issue that Assad is such a problem, we can't have a final resolution with his maintenance of power. Yet, we are also saying we need Russia to perform such a meaningful role in dealing with a resolution.

And Mr. Lister started along an area I wanted to pursue when he said Russians were at that airbase before the chemical weapons attack. And there were open source and unofficial reports that Russian-controlled drones were going over the hospital prior to the attack doing intelligence and recognizance, for what purpose, ahead of time. And how complicit is Russia, not just in their ignoring their responsibilities under the treaty that was negotiated in 2013, but complicit in some of these actions? As Dr. Rand said, it doesn't matter how people are killed. They were complicit in, you know I think, just the slaughter of civilians in their bombing and their military tactics, the same way working side-by-side with Assad.

So how can Russia be so pivotal in one sense to what we are doing, if they were complicit with Assad and Assad complicates this? If you can, delve into that. I know it is a difficult question but I appreciate all your thoughts on it.

Mr. LISTER. If I may, it is an excellent question, again, and an extremely important one. This is the meaty, horrible side of politics. Russia is our direct adversary in terms of Syria policy and yet, it is also part of the solution. It will have to be part of the solution. If it is not part of the solution, we won't get a solution.

The reason why I single out Russia as being part of that is largely because, as I said earlier, for Russia, Syria is something to be negotiated over. For Iran, this is zero-sum; there is nothing to negotiate.

So our only opening here is to convince the Russians that their current plan of action is unsustainable and it won't lead to the eventual objective that they want, which is, ultimately, ideally, for Assad to be still be in Damascus and in control of 100 percent of his territory. It is not going to happen.

We also need to bear in mind, in terms of your complicity question, Russia has a very different military philosophy. We saw, I believe in 1990, in its operation in Grozny in Chechnya, the idea of fighting terrorism for Russia was scorched earth. And this is precisely how Russia has further emboldened Assad's scorched earth policy. This is why I described the Syrian Army as a result of——

Mr. KEATING. And my time is running out but I think it is important to distinguish as well there is such a perception I think in our country that Russia is our ally targeting ISIS. And frankly, that is not the case there. Could you just maybe throw some of your knowledge that you have in this area toward at least breaking up that myth, to a degree?

Mr. LISTER. Sure. Well, I would be lying to say that Russia hasn't fought ISIS but I would be telling the truth to say it is far from their first priority.

Russia has pivoted on different priorities over time. When it has successfully negotiated with the international community to enforce a ceasefire between the opposition and the regime, it has then celebrated the success of having established a ceasefire, and then with all the world's media watching, pivoted to fight ISIS for a couple weeks.

Mr. KEATING. Well, thank you. My time is up. I would yield back but thank you for shedding some light on this.

Chairman ROYCE. We go to Mr. Joe Wilson of South Carolina.

Mr. WILSON. Thank you, Mr. Chairman, and I am very grateful for the leadership today of Chairman Ed Royce and Ranking Member Eliot Engel to hold a hearing as we discuss the long-term stability of not just Syria but the Middle East as a whole. And I am really pleased, too, how bipartisan this is. Indeed, I am happy to join with Congressman Greg Meeks to point out that we have a very insightful panel and I wish you well in your careers.

More than 500,000 people have been killed and 14 million driven from their homes as the result of the unending conflict. This gruesomely sad situation should have been dealt with earlier and I am disheartened that it has taken until a few weeks ago where action was taken against Assad after he conducted another chemical weapons attack, committing mass murder against his own people.

We find ourselves in a difficult situation today, as we have let Russia and Iran take an unnecessarily active role in shaping Syria's future. More should be done in Syria and more will be done.

I want to thank all of you for the testimony. For each of you, how do you assess the humanitarian crisis in Syria and the neighboring nations resolving itself? And I actually am trying to be positive. When we talk about a stable and prosperous Syria after the missile strikes, what you would you say are the most important milestones to achieve in order to incentivize millions of displaced Syrians to come home, beginning with Mr. Singh?

Mr. SINGH. Well thank you, Congressman. Thank you for your kind words.

It is a difficult question because I think we are actually quite far away from—and I appreciate you are trying to be optimistic but I think we are actually quite far away from any such milestones.

I do want to reiterate that while we talk quite a bit about Assad, and Russia, and Iran, and appropriately so, again, I think we need to bear in mind that this conflict is no longer sort of a single conflict and those actors, which are, I think, malign actors, are largely active in western Syria. And so you have these other quadrants of the conflict in which, for example, we wouldn't want to invite Assad, and the Russians, and the Iranians to have influence over the liberation of Raqqa and what is happening in eastern Syria.

I think what we need to do is to look at each of these quadrants separately, do what we can to stabilize each of them, and to empower local actors. And in doing so, perhaps return some semblance of stability to them, at least in the short-term preventing them from getting worse.

So as I look at southern Syria, for example, the Jordanians worry that renewed fighting in southern Syria, close to their border, where there is now an ISIS branch that has been established, could result in more refugee flows across their border. And as I said, they are already hosting up to upwards of a million refugees, which is a big strain. So at least preventing that from getting worse, I think, will be quite important.

Once we have achieved some measure of stability in one or more of those quadrants, then I think over the longer term you can think about how do you knit this back together. But I think the reality is, for the foreseeable future, you are not going to see Syria reunified. There is no single actor that has that capability and we shouldn't pursue that goal, first and foremost. It should be stability in these zones.

Mr. LISTER. Very briefly, I would say I would refer you to my full written testimony in which I do try to suggest, at least, and as I said in my opening comments, that there are interim things that we can do which I think can alleviate some of the very dire humanitarian situation. And there are things we can do with relatively minimal effort, although increasing investment from where we currently stand to allow refugees to come back into Syria, to allow interim reconstruction to begin. And all of that compiled together results in some indirect pressure on the Assad regime to consider negotiations in a serious way.

And I would encourage you to look, although it is far from perfect and certainly Turkey has problems in terms of being our ally at the moment, I would refer you to look at what was done in northern Aleppo and how effective, on a humanitarian level, that is now becoming. I would say 40,000 refugees have returned to that area now, which is, effectively, a safe zone, in the last 4 to 6 weeks or so. That gives us a signal of what is possible.

Ms. RAND. Thank you, Congressman. I would agree completely with my colleagues and just add two more very important points.

One, I think I mentioned earlier this access issue. There are five million or so Syrians living under opposition control or sort of non-regime control that are being denied access, it seems, to some of the humanitarian aid that even we are paying for. So the access issue, through the cross border, through Turkey, that is a key issue. That is a diplomatic issue. It is pushing our partners and pushing the Russians to help get this aid into Idlib Province and other provinces under the opposition control. So point number one is the access.

And second, to go back to the very good questions from your colleague from Massachusetts, you know the Russians are playing not only a scorched earth policy but their air war tactics are driving civilians from Syria in rapid numbers. And so they turn it on and off and they divert, as Mr. Lister said, to the ISIS fight for a moment and then go back to targeting.

But just in this month, I believe, the Russians have increased their targeting of civilians' Idlib homes and other places. And that really drives the refugee crisis because they are targeting hospitals. They are targeting civilian infrastructure sites. And that is what is making people leave their homes, when they are——

Mr. WILSON. Thank you, each of you.

Chairman ROYCE. Dr. Ami Bera.

Mr. BERA. Thank you, Mr. Chairman. I want to expand on something that my colleague, Mr. Keating, touched on. You know none
of us questions the measured response in response to the use of
chemical weapons. But at this juncture, we are given a task as
Members of Congress to start thinking about what next. And we
can't do that without—none of you speak on behalf of the administration. You are providing your opinion.

And let me just put that in context. When President Obama was
asking Congress to take actions, we had a hearing in this very committee in September 2013. And again, no disrespect to the panel,
but we had Secretary of Defense Hagel; we had Secretary of State
Kerry; and we had the chairman of the Joint Chiefs General
Dempsey, and we were able to ask those questions.

So let me remind the President that he doesn't have the authorization to take additional actions against Assad without consultation of Congress. And I know both the chairman and ranking member are doing their best to get those individuals from the administration in front of this committee but the President needs to understand that separation of powers and it is incredibly important.

Again, the measured response supported broadly by bipartisan
members here, but in isolation, that response of Tomahawk missiles doesn't accomplish anything. It is the what next.

And I appreciate the testimony of the witnesses. I think you are
providing valuable insight and opinion but we need the administration here so we can ask directly what their strategy is. And thus
far, the President hasn't stated what next strategy is and that is
a real concern.

You know, Dr. Rand, you touched on something and I think all
of you would agree on when we think about our foreign policy:
There are really three pillars here. There is certainly the defense
but then there is the diplomacy and the development aspects of foreign policy. And when we think about staffing levels at the State
Department, I am incredibly worried about our readiness for the
second and third pillars of whatever the next strategy is.

Dr. Rand, do you want to touch on the lack of staffing at State,
and the vulnerability, and our readiness here?

Ms. RAND. Thank you, Congressman for that question. First, I
should say that there are many, many dedicated career civil serv-
ants, and foreign service officers, and the majority of the State Department, USAID, who are there working day in and day out on
this issue, in particular. And I applaud their consistent contribu-
tion to this issue. It is a really tough tragedy to work on.

But yes, that is a concern. The way the State Department works
is that the political appointees who sit at the Deputy Assistant Secretary, Assistant Secretary level interact with their Department of
Defense colleagues to make sure that the three Ds are actually
working—the development, defense, and diplomacy—work syner-
gically together comprehensively. If you don't have those level of
appointees or those levels of leaders to go to the meetings and to
work with the military, you are inherently going to erode the con-
tributions at the civilian levels of U.N. foreign policy.

Mr. BERA. Great. Would either one of you want to comment?

Mr. SINGH. I just want to say one thing on this. I had spent some time myself at the State Department. I was a Special Assistant to Secretaries Powell and Rice. And I think that I agree with Dr. Rand on the principle that we need to get the State Department staffed up. We need to staff our diplomacy. I am concerned about some of the reports of big cuts to the State Department budget.

On the other hand, it is also important that we have the right organization at the State Department and, as I understand it, that is one of the things that Secretary Tillerson is looking at.

Because I think one lesson that I would take from the last administration is that we have to be careful that we have a unified Middle East strategy and that we empower our officials to look not just at one slice of the salami, as it were, but that we empower them to look at the entire region. So I would like to, for example, see an Assistant Secretary of State for Middle Eastern Affairs who actually has the power to look at multiple issues across the region and integrate them into a single strategy.

And I will also say my impression is, without minimizing your concerns, Congressman, that inside, for example, the National Security Council, the Trump administration is looking very carefully at this issue and what our strategy in Syria should be.

Mr. BERA. And again, I would just reiterate that may be taking place but there is a role for Congress and there is a role for that consultation with Congress. That is how our Government is set up.

And let me just say, not to minimize, we have great Government employees. We have great employees with the State, DoD, et cetera, that are doing a tremendous job.

So, again, I would just urge the administration to respect this committee. And I will yield back.

Chairman ROYCE. We go to Jeff Duncan of South Carolina.

Mr. DUNCAN. Thank you, Mr. Chairman.

You know we have a great panel. You guys are very well-versed in the topic. I just want to point out that we may have had some people from the administration here to testify, had some of the administration's appointments not been slow to be confirmed on the Senate side due to obstruction over there. And that is unfortunate because this is a very timely issue.

I want to speak on behalf of my constituents because I get a lot of messages to my office, Facebook, Twitter, other things that say this: What are the U.S. national security interests that are at stake in Syria and how do these Syria-specific interests relate to broader U.S. regional or global interests? What are we doing in Syria? Why is it important to the United States?

And I will start with Mr. Singh.

Mr. SINGH. Thank you, Congressman and it is a great question. And I think your constituents are absolutely right to ask that, as we should of every foreign policy issue.

I think we have several interests at stake here. Number one is counterterrorism, first and foremost, because obviously we are focused on defeating ISIS and trying to do it in a way which is sustainable, so that ISIS doesn't come back. And I think that is something that ordinary Americans are concerned about.

Second, we don't want to see Iran increase its power or increase its ability to project power, whether against our interests or against our allies like Israel and Jordan. And one thing that we have seen, as others have discussed, is that Iran is, in fact, attempting to do that.

There is also an element here where we have Russia trying to thwart American interests, American objectives in this region and project its own power globally.

And then just finally——

Mr. DUNCAN. Let me just ask you—I mean we tried that in Vietnam. How is this going to be different when we try to thwart another country like Russia's engagement in a certain region of the world? Can you touch on that?

Mr. SINGH. Well, I don't know that we are aiming to thwart Russia's engagement in this region of the world. As my colleague mentioned, Russia has had influence in Syria for a long time. I think it is actually reverse. I think Russia is trying to, in principle, prevent the United States from succeeding in this region. And that is a big concern, I think, for any policymaker, whatever your view of what a relationship with Russia should be in the long-run.

And I would just add one more thing, which is obviously we have seen this conflict cause tremendous instability in Europe. And instability in Europe is I think, also, a concern of the United States.

Mr. DUNCAN. Any of you others want to comment on that?

Mr. LISTER. I don't want to repeat what my colleague has said but I would want to reiterate the obvious is, of course, counterterrorism as an interest. We focused almost explicitly on ISIS for the last several years but we seem to have forgotten al-Qaeda. And that, for me in my area of work, is a very significant concern and we can come to that, perhaps with further questions.

The issue of international norms and American credibility is also at stake; I could speak at length at how American credibility has been severely damaged with regards to our treatment of the Syrian crisis over the last 6 years. And there are things, as my remarks said, that we can do to rescue some of that credibility.

Iran and Hezbollah are increasing like we have never seen them before. Hezbollah is now arguably more powerful than some Eastern European militaries.

Mr. DUNCAN. It is interesting that you mentioned that several times today about Iran and Hezbollah. Do you believe that Iran is emboldened based on the Iranian deal that gave them $400 billion plus that they could use to export terrorism to finance Hezbollah and other terrorist organizations? Do they feel more emboldened because they have the financial ability now from that deal?

Mr. LISTER. It is hard to say with certainty, although, I would find it hard to believe they didn't find themselves feeling more emboldened. I think the one key difference I can tell after the JCPOA in terms of Iran's strategy in Syria is that they have managed to train these Shia militiamen from all across the region, and far more intensively, and far more professionally than they were before. Whereas, we saw 2 or 3 years ago tens of thousands compiled of Afghan Hazara Shia militiamen essentially being cannon fodder in strategic areas. They are now highly capable forces. And that can only have been the result of increased funding, logistical support, training facilities, and of course, travel across the region.

Mr. DUNCAN. I know Dr. Rand wants to get in here and I have 30 seconds but let me just make a point and ask Dr. Rand. Do you think if the United States hadn't pulled out of Iraq prematurely without leaving a contingency there, things would be different in western Iraq and Syria?

Ms. RAND. Thank you, Congressman.

You know the Iraq point is a very good one and I actually would disagree slightly that the Shia militia training, the cause and effect of that probably predates the JCPOA. It probably goes back many, many years. I mean you could date it even to 2006-2007, when these Shiite militias were forming.

So I don't think it is the 2011-2010 period that we are talking about. I think we are talking—if you want to cite Iraq as a causal variable that led to the growth of the Shiite militia movement and their ability to train and seize power, I would go even earlier to 2005, 2006, 2007.

Mr. DUNCAN. My time is up.

Mr. Chairman, I reiterate it would be nice to have some administration officials here.

Chairman ROYCE. Very good.

Dina Titus of Nevada.

Ms. TITUS. Thank you, Mr. Chairman. I am afraid I am going to be saying the same thing that most of my colleagues have said because I share their sentiments.

I think the meandering policies of the Trump administration have done nothing to end the civil war in Syria. We all agree it is a complicated situation. That is why we need a clear strategy with a focused execution and leadership and that is not what we have. The only thing this administration has been clear about is that Assad, apparently, gets to stay in power and he is the person who has been willing to kill more 500,000 of his own people.

We haven't received any details about how the President wants to work with others in the area. We haven't seen this super-secret plan to get rid of ISIS. All we have seen are some so-called messages that have been sent to Iran and North Korea. And we have had the mother of all bombs dropped. We have had the Armata going somewhere; we don't know where. We have had saber-rattling that has upset some of our closest allies. It seems to me a kind of mass confusion and it is very unpredictable, which means it is unstable and can lead to mistakes.

In the meantime, the State Department has been sidelined in the whole process of forming any kind of cohesive foreign policy strategy.

I will agree with Mr. Keating, Dr. Bera, Mr. Duncan, you all are wonderful. You are the experts, obviously, but we have had nobody from the administration. Your analysis is interesting to us but you are think tank people. You are academics. You are former administration folks. You are not who is there now and supposed to be making the decisions.

I know we are trying to get the Secretary here. Maybe we need to get Ivanka here—she has her brother whispering that she is the one who suggested they do the bombing—or Jared Kushner. Maybe they are the ones doing the policy. So maybe we need to bring them in front of us and ask them what is going on.

In the meantime, I would just ask Dr. Rand, you know it has been 20 days since we dropped all the missiles on Syria. Now, President Trump all the time has said I will never forecast what I am going to do. Unlike the previous administration, I am not going to warn the enemy. Well, they warned Russia and they high-tailed it out of there. Russia warned Syria; they got out of there. They were using the airfield the very next day. Those precious babies that so moved our President when they were hit with the chemical gas are still being killed by barrel bombs or are washing up on the shores of Greek islands because they are refugees.

What was the effect of that, that message? What good did it do? Doctor, do you see any effect on the regime of that strike? Would you advise doing more strikes, less strikes, what?

Ms. RAND. Yes, thank you Congresswoman. Three weeks later, it is hard to say exactly what the impact was in terms of the civil conflict, in terms of the war against ISIS, and in terms of our allies. I think there were a lot of raised hopes and expectations among many allies in many different parts of the world. And the neighbors had different views, as I said, and they read into the strikes what they want U.S. policy to be, which often conflicts with each other, which is of concern.

But no, I didn't see a deterrent effect in terms of slowing down Assad's killing machine, nor slowing down Russian support for Assad in the past 3 weeks.

Ms. TITUS. So the message wasn't very clear or wasn't very effective?

Ms. RAND. Yes, I don't think that message had that sort of impact.

Ms. TITUS. Mr. Lister?

Mr. LISTER. The message was clear in one single act but there is no strategy. The only impact I can say that we have seen is that there clearly is still some concern within the Assad regime about the fact that we did conduct the attack because they have redeployed almost of their aircraft to Russia's military base in the northwest of the country for protection.

So clearly, the impact of one strike of 59 cruise missiles has made people ask questions about whether or not we will do it again but they shouldn't just be asking the questions. It should be clear from our side whether or not there will be any more or whether there will not be.

So clearly, as I said in my opening remarks, we do need an underpinning strategy to have the proper effect that we want.

Ms. TITUS. All right.

Mr. SINGH. You know I confess I disagree slightly with my colleagues on this. I think of the narrow purpose of these strikes was to deter the use of chemical weapons and to lend credibility to American military threats, I think that it is possible that they will succeed in that narrow basis but, again, that is narrow. So I wouldn't be quite as negative about it, perhaps, as you suggest.

Ms. TITUS. I think that you say it is possible that it will succeed. What happens if it doesn't deter them and they do it again? That is the big question that looms out there. What next, I guess, is the point.

Thank you, Mr. Chairman. I yield back.

Chairman ROYCE. Scott Perry of Pennsylvania.

Mr. PERRY. Thanks, Mr. Chairman.

As is often the case in this committee, I feel like I am compelled to correct the record by the time it comes to my opportunity to ask some questions. So I am just going to take some time to remind everybody who says that we must have a strategy and that this side opposes such a thing, nothing could be further from the truth. We believe that we must have a strategy and that the President must come to us as well for further and continued military action.

That having been said, let's just be reminded that he has been in office for about 100 days. Meanwhile, for 8 years prior to this, we still didn't see a strategy and, when we did, well it was a red line, and then I am going to take some military action, and then when the American people disagree with it, then I am going to go to the Congress, and then I am not going to do anything. And if this is complicated, which it is, I would say that whatever the strategy was during the last administration has a lot to do with the complications we are dealing with right now, which includes Russian involvement, which the United States effectively kept out of the Middle East for 60 years under previous policy. Let's not forget that.

All right, moving on. Does anybody on the panel believe that Moscow was aware of Assad's use of chemical weapons beforehand and/or approved of it or was it beyond its control, Russia? Mr. Singh, do you know?

Mr. SINGH. I don't know but it is hard for me to imagine that Russia and Iran wouldn't be aware of those types of things, given the integration between these militaries.

Mr. PERRY. Mr. Lister?

Mr. LISTER. Just to add briefly, the French Government released an investigation into the attack yesterday. They actually deployed assets to the town that was attacked.

One of the things they found was the chemical hexamine was used as a mixing agent for sarin. The key thing about hexamine is it takes many, many hours, if not 1 to 2 days, to actually complete the process of forming sarin. It is composed of—it is a binary chemical.

Mr. PERRY. Right.

Mr. LISTER. There have been media reports here in the United States citing unnamed intelligence officials saying that we had detected people linked to the chemical weapons program going to the Shayrat Air Base in the days preceding the attack. If those reports are true and we indeed did detect those things, there is no way in my mind that Russia, having troops on the base itself, could not have known.

Mr. PERRY. Wouldn't know. Wouldn't know, right.

So it would seem that Russia, potentially, at least at this point, could be complicit and it seems to be pointing in that direction.

Dr. Rand, do you have a countervailing opinion?

Ms. RAND. Well I agree. I think actually the most guilty behavior was afterwards, where there was a disinformation campaign in the weeks subsequent, where Russia was denying this attack to place in the face of the hospital reports from Turkey, the——

Mr. PERRY. Overwhelming evidence.

Ms. RAND. Yes. So that actually, I don't know the answer to your question but that was pretty damning.

Mr. PERRY. To what extent can Assad defy Russia? I mean they are trying to influence. They have their base there. They want to keep Assad to that extent but I would agree they are looking for stability that they are not going to get. What kind of leash does he have? Does he have a pretty broad range of authority where he can still receive compliance from Russia and things like what we just discussed, potentially?

Mr. SINGH. That is an awfully tough question to answer, Congressman. I think he, as Charles mentioned, he needs Russia and Iran, especially, to have any hope of success militarily in the battlefield. At the same time, they need him. There is no Assad regime without Assad.

Mr. PERRY. Right.

Mr. SINGH. So there is a codependency. And exactly what is the dynamic in that relationship, I would be hard-pressed to say.

Mr. PERRY. But I would think, at a minimum, we are hard-pressed to put a whole lot or really any degree of trust in Russia in some kind of bilateral operations or negotiations. I mean we are forced to it because they are at the table because the last administration essentially allowed them at the table or they forced themselves to the table. But we can't trust them in anything we are doing. Would that be a fair assessment?

Mr. SINGH. I think that our history of negotiations so far have shown that, as Mr. Lister mentioned, they have a pretty poor track record when it comes to enforcing ceasefires and getting Assad to do what he needs to do.

Mr. PERRY. Just looking further, what would their objective be in Libya and Egypt? Is this the beginning of further influence in the region?

Mr. SINGH. Well I think, broadly, Russia is trying to reassert itself as a global power. It is trying to reestablish its influence in regions like the Middle East but not only the Middle East. And look, having a presence there on NATO's southern flank, you know they obviously have quite a presence on NATO's eastern flank, gives them a bit of influence and leverage over especially those southern NATO countries.

So I think that there are a lot of different things in play.

Mr. PERRY. Yes, so I think we need to be wary of that and aware of that.

Regarding future negotiations and stability, and your assertion that it is not going to come anytime soon, and I would agree with you, are there decision points for Russia? And if there are, and I imagine there are, do you have any inclination to what they would be?

And finally, Mr. Chairman, with your indulgence, would you just acknowledge that it was protocol to allow the Russians to know that our missiles indeed were inbound. It was not collaboration or collusion, it is protocol.

Mr. SINGH. It is protocol and I think it is prudence, as well, frankly.

Mr. PERRY. Okay. And the previous question?

Mr. SINGH. The decision points for Russia.

Mr. PERRY. Yes.

Mr. SINGH. Russia is obviously most active in that western sort of quadrant of the conflict, as well as a bit in the southern quadrant. And it seems right now they are trying to establish control around Idlib.

And so I think that seems to be the focus but I think whether or not that remains the focus, how that goes will depend also in part on what happens in the rest of the country. I think, for example, a successful operation to liberate Raqqa changes the sort of facts on the ground because it really, especially if we are starting to empower local actors there, it eliminates the possibility that Assad can somehow regain control of the country and perhaps changes the dynamics for Russia, for Assad, for Iran.

Chairman ROYCE. Thank you. We go to Brad Schneider, Brad Schneider of Illinois.

Mr. SCHNEIDER. Thank you, Mr. Chairman and thank you, again, for calling this hearing. To the witnesses, your testimony, your written testimony in particular, was extraordinarily helpful.

I want to associate myself with my colleagues about the need for a strategy, the need for the administration to be here speaking to us. But also I want to, as maybe starting a trend, set the record straight because it was indicated that it is obstruction that is slowing down having people in place. And I just want to point out that there have been very few nominations made within the State Department, among other departments.

There are two upcoming nomination hearings. The Senate is moving quickly. We need the senior officials to be nominated and in place to make sure that we implement the strategy we need to have in place.

Moving to questions, Mr. Lister, you indicated in your testimony that Assad cannot put Syria back together again. Is that a statement about Assad or is it more a statement about Syria in general?

Mr. LISTER. I take it to mean the latter part of your question is implying whether partition is possible?

Mr. SCHNEIDER. No, the question is can Syria be put together again or is it something that we are trying to do the impossible? Mr.

LISTER. Fundamentally speaking, a very significant propor- tion of Syria's population have seen the wrath of the Assad regime and the methods he uses—so the Assad regime's chief motto is Assad or we burn the country. Assad frequently says he is cleansing his country of the impure.

With Assad still in place and with his foreign intelligence apparatus, you have every single piece of information about anyone who could potentially be opposed to his regime. While he stays in power, six and a half million Syrians will never go back.

Mr. SCHNEIDER. And I agree that Assad can't. But is it possible to put Syria back together at this point?

Mr. LISTER. I think so, yes, in the long-term. The key thing for everyone to bear in mind is that the only thing, in my experience, that unites the opposition and the regime is an opposition to Syria falling apart. Both of them oppose partition 100 percent.

Mr. SCHNEIDER. Good.

Mr. Singh, turning to you. You talked about Syria being a conflict spread over four zones. And as I look at it and others were talking about it, it is maybe more. There are more facets to this challenge.

But I wonder is it one conflict over four zones or it is four conflicts with intersections, or using Mr. Lister's term, interlinked conflicts?

Mr. SINGH. Congressman, I mean I guess you would apply almost either terminology to it. I think the point, from my point of view, is that you can't treat Syria as one problem, in a sense. In fact, you have distinct but, perhaps, overlapping problems. So for example, we have the problem that has erupted in recent days of the Turks and the Kurds in their tensions to one another and clashes with one another now. We have the problem of Iran and Hezbollah trying to establish a presence along the Golan Heights. We have the problem, potentially, of, if there is renewed fighting in the south, refugees flowing into Jordan and the Jordanians feeling as though they have to do something perhaps to push ISIS back from their own borders.

And then we also have the sort of issue that really we are focused on in this hearing of western Syria and the plight of civilians who are caught between the Assad regime and its backers and the opposition which is, as I said, increasingly jihadist dominated in that area.

So these are all sort of parts of the Syrian conflict but I think that to make good policy, we may need to look at them not separately, not totally distinctly, but as sort of discrete problems, if you know what I mean.

Mr. SCHNEIDER. Dr. Rand, I don't know if you have comments to add to that.

Ms. RAND. Concurring.

Mr. SCHNEIDER. Okay. As I try to understand what is happening and, again, thank you for sharing your insights, it seems that we need to have certainly a multi-faceted strategy, if not overlaying strategies that are distinct.

On the one level, we have this humanitarian crisis that we have to deal with with, not just the internally displaced but the pressure it is putting on the region.

Mr. Singh, as you touched on, we have the regional issues in what is happening at the north along the Turkish borders is distinct from what is happening on the highway between Damascus and Aleppo, distinct from what is happening near the Golan. And having that tragedy on the regional and then the global, we are running out of time, but the issue of the prospect of a failed state in Iraq being a haven for terrorist groups and, Mr. Lister, thank you for emphasizing al-Qaeda because it is not just ISIS. We have to have a strategy with all of those.

So I guess I am going to finish with a statement for a question because I am out of time. But it is imperative that we have the administration here sharing with us, so that Congress can exercise its responsibility to understand and ultimately make the decision of what role the United States should be playing in these conflicts.

So with that, I yield back. Thank you very much.

Chairman ROYCE. Thank you for those questions.

We will now go to Chairman McCaul from Texas.

Mr. MCCAUL. All right, thank you, Chairman.

My first question is to Mr. Lister and maybe for the panel. I have been briefed on this Democratic Federation of Northern Syria that operates, obviously, in the northern part of the country. On December 29th, the 165 leaders, Kurdish, Christian, Yazidi, and Arab populations came together to form a counsel and declare the creation of a government known as the Democratic Federation of Northern Syria. And it was sort of intriguing to me. I know some of our Special Forces may be working with them to defeat ISIS but what intrigued me about this group was that, at some point, if and when Assad falls, we are going to have to have some model of governance, some template for the country. And I think that is something that we have seen historically in the past we have made mistakes on, when a dictator falls and there is no governance, then the terrorists take over.

And so my question is can you tell me more about this Federation and the prospects of it and other groups like it becoming sort of a model governance?

Mr. LISTER. Sure. Well, the formation you speak of is essentially a result of the Kurdish YPG's policy in northeastern Syria, which is to establish a semi-autonomous region of the country either with or without the tacit acceptance of the United States and with or without the tacit acceptance of the Assad regime, both of whom it retains contact with.

You know many of the underpinning philosophies underpinning it are good and laudable. The idea of freedom of representation, in theory, the theory of equal opportunities for the sexes is all good, and there are many, many more. There are problems with it, though, within this Federation territory, it has become all the more common now for any portions of opposition or any other Kurdish parties that aren't the YPG have had their offices raided, burnt down, arrested. It is now illegal, according to that Federation for any of the leaders of those other Kurdish parties to even enter the territory.

So it is potentially a good stabilizing measure in the interim period but it isn't part of a solution I can see other Syrians and the rest of the country being part of.

Mr. MCCAUL. Is it something the United States should be supporting?

Mr. LISTER. In the interim, perhaps, yes, I mean because it works for now. It has stabilized northeastern Syria. It has resulted in the defeat of ISIS in those areas. But we need to be very, very aware of how poisonous, and I use that word, how poisonous the YPG's political philosophy is perceived by Syrians on both sides of the opposition-regime conflict. There are significant fears.

I will end just by saying I was part of a significant Track II process for 3 years, which involved almost a thousand Syrians from across all sides of the conflict, highly influential people in their own regard. The only actor not involved in that process was the PYD, the political wing of the YPG. And the only reason for that is nearly every single Syrian involved in that process said they would boycott the process if the PYD was involved.

It is just worth us remembering that using that as a model for the rest of Syria will not work, whilst it may work in the northeast. But it is not translatable for the rest of the country.

Mr. McCAUL. Well, following on the YPG, on Tuesday, Turkey launched an airstrike against groups, Kurds, including the YPG in Syria. We have been working with them to defeat ISIS. I know there were communications to Turkey not to do this. The President is meeting with President Erdogan next month.

As a member of NATO, how do you propose that the United States balance this issue?

Mr. LISTER. Well, I would refer you to my earlier testimony and to my prepared remarks. I refer to the fact that Turkey has many faults but also we have many faults with this situation.

We have pretended that the YPG isn't part of the PKK, which is a designated terrorist organization in this country. The PKK is also the primary national security threat for Turkey and it has been for 30 or 40 years.

So there are things we do need to do to build confidence back up with the Turks and the primary policy recommendation I would have there in the immediate term is to try to encourage or force Turkey to reconsider a ceasefire with the PKK inside Turkey, which would then have the positive knock-on effect of de-intensifying the hostilities between Turkey and the YPG.

For me, that is the only way around it.

Mr. McCAUL. I assume the other witnesses agree with this assessment?

Ms. RAND. Yes, this is exactly right. I would just add that the President and the new administration seem to be trying to warm relationships with Turkey. There were a number of phone calls, including after the referendum 10 days ago, congratulating President Erdogan. This is a new warm relationship that has to be translated into tough talk and negotiations on these types of issues to promise to work on the YPG issue in exchange for restraint and not to target people that our Special Forces are working with and partnering with.

Mr. McCAUL. Thank you. I see my time has expired.

Chairman ROYCE. Thank you for those questions.

We will now go to Mr. Espaillat from New York.

Mr. ESPAILLAT. Thank you, Mr. Chairman, Ranking Member Engel. And esteemed witnesses, thank you for your excellent and enlightening testimony.

I don't mean to pile on but, however, thus far, so far in Congress and with full control of both the Senate, the House, and the White House, it is perplexing that we have not heard from a State Department official who might really play a constructive role in answering some of the questions that we may have.

Just yesterday we heard from Secretary of State Tillerson and General Mattis on the North Korea issue. And we have not used military force there, yet. So I think it is imperative that we hear from the administration on their plan, their strategic long-term plan to address this humanitarian crisis in Syria. Close to half a million civilians have died or exactly 480,000, and 14 million people have been displaced, and maybe 50 or more percent of the country's infrastructure has been destroyed.

So this is truly a humanitarian crisis and beyond the attack on the airfield, we have not really heard from the President or his administration on the long-term strategic plan to deal with this particular humanitarian crisis. And we saw how while he warned the Russians of the planned military action, he ordered the launch of 59 Tomahawks on Shayrat Airfield in Syria. And he very emotionally and appropriately stated that Assad choked out the lives of helpless, men, women, and children. It was a slow and brutal death for many of them.

But less than 24 hours after the attack, the Syrian Government and their Russian allies were able to continue to fly missions out of the airfield. When will they fly another mission with chemical weapons? That is the question that we must all ask ourselves. In fact, there are recent allegations that even after the airfield attack, the regime has used chlorine gas against civilians.

And so we want to know, I want to ask is there any evidence? Have you heard of any evidence of this being true that they have, in fact, after the sarin attack, they have used other chemical weapons on the Syrian people?

Mr. LISTER. Briefly, yes, or as much evidence as we can glean without being there ourselves. Doctors on the ground have treated chlorine-like symptoms, difficulty breathing, tearing from the eyes in, as far as I am aware, at least three different locations since our cruise missile strikes, including one of the times which was literally the day after our cruise missile strike. And those attacks are taking place just outside Damascus and elsewhere in the north of the country.

Mr. ESPAILLAT. So the bombing of the airfield has not deterred the Assad regime from continuing in its bad ways. And so we must hear from the administration on the strategic long-term plan in the region. The President, in his first 100 days has issued executive orders to a 4-month halt on allowing refugees in to the United States. We just heard in the past days how his assistant and First Daughter Ivanka contradicted that particular policy, saying that allowing Syrian refugees into the United States has to be part of the discussion. Maybe we should allow that statement into the record, Mr. Chairman, but we must continue to highlight America's long-standing tradition to offer humanitarian aid and allow refugees from troubled parts of the world to enter America, where they will protected and shielded from bodily harm. This is an important component of who we are as a nation and we must continue to look in that direction.

Trump is proposing cuts on the State Department and we heard how General Mattis has stated that if we cut diplomacy, we just buy additional bullets. And so we are in the crossroad where we have not heard from the administration with proposing cuts on the State Department, the Assad regime continues to violate human rights. We are not clear on where we are going and yet, we are not speaking to each other. And we speak to each other about North Korea, as we should and yet, we have not used physical force there. So we must continue to support refugees coming in. We have a good vetting system to ensure that they are not here to harm our nation. And whether they are children being killed in El Salvador, Guatemala, Honduras, or Syria, they are children that we should help across the world.

And I am asking President Trump to reverse his course on the executive order and to come to Congress with a long-term foreign policy strategy on Syria.

Thank you, Mr. Chairman.

Mr. YOHO [presiding]. Thank you, sir. It is now my turn and so I am going to ask you guys, and I appreciate your patience being here. I want to go back to the subject of this hearing, Syria After the Missile Strikes: Policy Options.

I was torn when President Trump ordered those Tomahawk missiles in there because I was a strong opponent of President Obama going in there when they were going to do the no-fly zones because was saw what happens with no-fly zones in Libya. It leads to a failed state. There is nobody to take over and that was our concern back then. And this was a limited strike.

And I want to go back to some of the stuff that you said. Mr. Lister, you said you noted that the mode of death—whether it is bombs, bullets, I threw in beheading, or chemicals—it is still death but the chemical weapons have been deemed an unacceptable form of warfare. And if we go back to the Chemical Weapons Convention, it comprehensibly prohibits the use, the development, the production, stockpiling, and transfer of chemical weapons. Any chemical used for warfare is considered a chemical weapon by the Convention. And then we have the chlorine barrel bombs that Assad has been using. And we have written bills to prevent that. We can't get the traction because everybody says chlorine is not considered a use but within the chemical weapons treaty it says the use of any toxic chemical as a weapon, when used to produce fatalities solely or majoritively through its toxic action is in and of itself forbidden by the treaty.

So my question to you is: We have pretty much every country in the world signed on to the CWC and there are four of them that haven't. So the consensus is, with all the countries, the 192 that have agreed to this, is that chemical weapons should not be used. So we are in agreement there.

Is there an enforcement mechanism or is it just an agreement we are not going to use them? And if somebody crosses that red line and uses them, is there an international response written down anywhere and, if not, would you recommend there should be and it should be an international coalition of all nations?

What are your thoughts, Mr. Singh?

Mr. SINGH. Well, Congressman, thanks for the question. I confess I am not an expert in the CWC. So I am not sure I have the answer to your questions.

But I think if the treaty is going to mean anything and it is a lesson also for other nonproliferation treaties, which we put a lot of emphasis on, there have to be sanctions. There have to be penalties for those who violate them and it can't be just American penalties and American sanctions. It needs to be international.

Mr. YOHO. And that is what I want to come out of this so that it gives clarity for a nation because I don't want America to have to do this alone but after 5 years of slaughter over there and pushing 500,000 people and, as Ms. Titus brought up, you know this administration has done nothing. Well, we can blame a lot of administrations for not doing anything. And we need to have the clarification of if this does happen and we have signed on to these agreements, somebody needs to back them up.

Mr. Lister, do you have any thoughts on that?

Mr. LISTER. I am also not an expert on the treaty either or the Convention and I would echo what Mr. Singh has said. It is our responsibility as an international community to enforce conventions like this.

Mr. YOHO. All right, and I know you guys aren't the experts or want to talk about the policy side of that but you are experts in your fields. So I am asking you to give us the information that you would draft as far as a wording that we could go to the U.N. and say we want this or go to our State Department and say we want this wording put into the international community that if you cross this red line, not just America, but all the members that have signed up to this are coming after you.

Dr. Rand? And Mr. Lister you said—you looked like you had something else to add.

Mr. LISTER. I will just finish. I think the responsibility to protect is a useful mechanism here. If chemical weapons are proven to be being used against civilian populations repeatedly, that may give us one opportunity under some kind of a U.N. mandate to at least push for some kind of response and consequences for it.

Yes, that is what I would offer.

Mr. YOHO. Dr. Rand?

Ms. RAND. I would agree with the RTP, the responsibility to protect method of advancing this but I would also add that you know last week at the U.N. there was a resolution, or 2 weeks ago right after the missile strikes, to condemn it and to investigate it and Russia vetoed it, in fact, on the one paragraph on the information about they didn't like the way it was worded or something. But I think the main diplomatic task ahead is to go back on this particular strike and ensure that there is an investigation because that is part of the norm against CW is the international community goes in, and investigates, and holds accountable individuals, including by name, by the way. The PCW has been very good at finding the perpetrators in the past 2 years.

Mr. YOHO. Right.

Ms. RAND. It has a published list of names.

Mr. YOHO. And my goal is that we have an enforcement mechanism that has teeth behind it because that is the only way I could justify what President Trump did is the slaughter that has been going on for over 5 years, that it has to be brought to an end. And if we just sit by as a world, we are all guilty of watching this happen. And so I am glad he stepped in but before we go any further, we need to have clarification.

And my time is out.

And we will go now to Mr. Brad Sherman from California.

Mr. SHERMAN. Thank you.

We have three separate goals in Syria and there is a tendency to mash them together. We have to keep them separate, evaluating every policy as to whether it helps at least one of those goals without setting back one of the others. And we shouldn't attack a proposal just because it does nothing to achieve two of our goals if it, in fact, helps us achieve one of the three goals.

Our first goal is to protect the Syrian people and we would, eventually, like to see good governance in Syria. Our second goal is to destroy ISIS. And our third goal is to preserve the Chemical Weapons Convention that bans the use of poison gas.

And there has been discussion here about how the mode of death doesn't matter. You are just as dead if you are hit by a bullet or a bomb as if you are hit with sarin. But the fact is that we live in a world in which mankind at least achieved the Chemical Weapons Convention.

One could write an account or history where chemical weapons were invented before gunpowder and in that account or history, chemical weapons are allowed and explosives are not but that is not the way history unfolded. We have a convention against the use of chemical weapons that has saved countless millions of lives and it is worth standing up for that convention, even if we realize that Assad has killed half a million people, or the war that he created has killed half a million people, and only a very, very small percentage of those died from chemical weapons.

Now not only do we have those three goals, the Syrian people, ISIS, and the Chemical Weapons Convention, they are not equally important goals, but we have a couple of caveats. And that is we want to do that all without excessive U.S. casualties and without a war with Russia. We don't want another Iraq War. We don't want another Cuban Missile Crisis.

Now, one of our colleagues said that he thought that there was a moral equivalence between Assad and other authoritarian regimes in the Middle East. I would say Mubarak did not kill hundreds of thousands of people. In fact, he allowed himself to be, or was allowed to leave power, rather than killing hundreds of thousands.

Not every authoritarian regime in the Middle East is responsible for aiding the killing of hundreds of Americans, as Mr. Lister pointed out, the Assad regime is.

Not every Middle East authoritarian regime has tried to develop nuclear weapons the way Syria did until they were bombed in 2007, and no doubt they paid North Korea for the material and the technology. So, they proliferated in that direction as well. That is money in the hands of North Korea.

And there are 500,000 dead Syrians. That does not equate to Erdogan. And I have been one of the harshest critics of Erdogan on this committee.

The Obama administration forced Assad to give up 2,600 pounds of chemical weapons. That was a tremendous accomplishment. And our hope is that the action taken by President Trump will prevent Assad from using whatever he has left. We will have to see.

There is discussion of chlorine versus other chemical agents. It is my understanding that the Chemical Weapons Convention would prohibit Syria from even possessing sarin and other chemical agents. They are allowed to possess chlorine. You can't have a modern society without chlorine and chlorinated water but it prohibits the use of chlorine as a weapon.

And of course when chlorine is used, you can't always be sure it was the Assad regime. Chlorine is a much more available item and the rebels, or the terrorists, or others might have it.

The question I have requires an understanding of Russian politics. So if I don't see a volunteer, maybe you could comment for the record. And that is, there is, among other things in the Middle East, a civil war between Shiites and Sunnis. The Russians have adopted the Shiites. Their own Muslim population is overwhelmingly Sunni. How does Putin, the man who at least asserts that his hold on power is dependent upon the consent of the government, side with the Shiites in this effort without an incredible blowback? We all have ethnic and religious communities in our districts and I doubt that we would fail to take into account their historical view in looking at international affairs.

Does anybody have a comment on how and why Putin can side with the Shiites when he has tens of millions of Sunnis?

Mr. LISTER. Very briefly, just academically, I would push back on the idea that Syria, at least within the frame of reference of Syria, that it is all just about Shiite versus Sunni. There are many Sunnis who have remained loyal to the Assad regime, just as many have turned to the opposition. And Russia has actually tried to frame it that way.

Mr. SHERMAN. But Hezbollah and Iran are there supporting Assad out of a Shiite——

Mr. LISTER. Exactly but Russia has tried to frame its policy in Syria domestically as not being protecting the Shia.

It is also worth remembering one thing that is going on right now which is having very little media coverage, in Aleppo city, having captured it, the Russian Government is now trying very hard to prevent Iran and the Assad regime from populating eastern Aleppo, which was previously under the opposition control. It is trying to prevent them from populating that area with Shia. And it is insisting that Sunnis, including from opposition areas, should be given the opportunity to come back to eastern Aleppo.

And so I would remind you that it is a little more complicated, domestically and also on Syrian than the binary——

Mr. KINZINGER [presiding]. The gentleman's time has expired. I thank the gentleman.

The Chair recognizes the Chair for 5 minutes.

I just want to dispel very quickly—there is a lot of talk about nonintervention in Syria and using Libya as the example. I think it is really important to point out that Libya has massive challenges. Part of that was a failure in follow-up after regime change, I believe.

But secondly, if you compare the case of intervention in Libya versus the case of nonintervention in Syria, Libya, with all its challenges, is far better off than not intervened—in Syria.

I remember back in 2013 I was one of the few Republicans outspoken about the need to enforce the red line in Syria. And I heard from people all over, a lot in my own party, some members on this committee, that said if we intervene and we strike Syria, we will begin World War III, and another major intervention in Syria, in the Middle East, World War III will commence and everybody will be gone.

I would like to point out that also people said that if we intervened, it will get way worse in Syria. But when we didn't intervene, it actually got way worse than we ever could have imagined, which is where we are at today.

So as we look at going forward and we imagine all the terrible possibilities and probably most of them are terrible, I would like to remind people that I think it can get even worse than it is right now, which is almost unimaginable.

As Mr. Lister mentioned in his statement, a very important thing happened after the strike on the airbase in Syria, which is the people who sat around said what are the Russians going to do, they got their question answered, which is absolutely nothing. They do not have the ability to respond, to react. Russia is not the former Soviet Union. It is a military where half of its planes can't even fly and it is very underfunded. So I think that is important to note, too, as we look at what we are going to do going forward.

Mr. Lister, let me ask a question. What is Bashar al-Assad's ultimate fear? What is the one thing that, if we push on that button, would drive President Assad, Dictator Assad, to the table to negotiate?

Mr. LISTER. My theory would be his ultimate fear is America gets really serious about Syria and not just about ISIS.

The only substantive evidence I can recall for that is back in August 2013, after the chemical weapons attack, in the brief period of time where it looked like the United States may conduct limited punitive strikes, I knew Syrians who were in Damascus at the time on the government side who said that nearly half of the Syrian Parliament packed up their homes and fled to Lebanon because they feared that limited, very limited American military action was going to set forth a chain of events that would have completely caused chaos within the regime, not the state, but the regime's inner circles.

So the biggest fear for Assad isn't terrorism. In fact, he has used terrorism for his own means, not just during this crisis but before, his biggest fear is that we get serious about solving Syria. And he has enjoyed the last 6 years because we haven't.

Mr. KINZINGER. So would you say that ultimately he fears his own life in that process? So if he would lose power in the regime, or his life, or whatever, that is what can be used as a trigger point to drive to a negotiated solution because short of that, short of any fear of losing power, he has no incentive whatsoever to negotiate an end to this war on anything but his own terms.

So I guess my point is, as the administration goes forward, they ought to look at using further air strikes against regime targets as a method to drive a negotiated solution here, as the diplomatic instrument of power against an adversary can only be effective when backed by the military instrument of power. We see that in North Korea. We see that here.

Let me ask you another question. Can Bashar al-Assad ever gain ultimate control of all of Syria again? I mean short of the entire world backing his regime, can he ever gain control of Syria?

Mr. LISTER. You can't discount anything but if he is going to militarily conquer the rest of his country, it is going to take a very, very, very long time, and it is going to cause a huge further exodus of civilians and many, many more deaths, and it could take 10, 20, 30 years to do so.

So, the real answer is, effectively, no if the answer is that he is then putting the country back together again. You know, it is essentially that.

Mr. KINZINGER. So without a strategy against Assad, be it negotiated or otherwise, you see part of regime controlled territory and you see a large part of the country, which is Afghanistan pre-9/11, basically, with some terrorist groups, some opposition groups running around.

So what would Assad staying in power, very briefly because my time is up, what does that do to the al-Qaeda affiliate in Syria?

Mr. LISTER. Okay, as fast as possible. Al-Qaeda has spent the last 6 years embedding itself in an opposition narrative in Syria. It has devoted all of its resources to fighting Assad, not creating an Islamic State, not fighting a transnational jihad. And for that reason only, the continued existence of Assad in Damascus and his continued brutality against his people, every single day emboldens al-Qaeda's narrative in the eyes of other Syrians who don't buy into a transnational jihad. And this is the fear: Every single day more and more people think, huh, maybe this group has got it right. They have always told us the international community will never come to our aid. So because they are right, because they are there, because they are powerful on the battlefield, maybe these are the guys that we should be joining. And that is the state where we are today.

Mr. KINZINGER. Thank you. My time has expired.

I think it is Mr. Cicilline from Rhode Island.

Mr. CICILLINE. Thank you, Mr. Chairman. And thank you to the chairman and ranking member for calling this hearing. Thank you to our witnesses.

It has been 3 weeks since President Trump launched a missile attack against the Assad regime and we are no closer to achieving a solution to this crisis. The Trump administration has not formulated any coherent policy to address ISIS or the ongoing atrocities being committed against the Syrian people by Bashar al-Assad.

In actuality, the inconsistency and confusion displayed by members of the Trump administration has emboldened Assad and his patron, Vladimir Putin. A monstrous chemical weapons attack deployed against innocent civilians, including women and children, came just days after Secretary of State Tillerson signaled to Assad and Putin that the United States was willing to accept Assad's continued role, which represented a stark turnaround from previous American policy.

And in the meantime, President Trump continues to push for his cruel and unnecessary ban on Syrian refugees, as well as draconian cuts to our foreign affairs budget. Each of these actions will only worsen the suffering of the Syrian people and that is why I, along with Congressman Beyer and Congresswoman Jayapal, are leading a letter to President Trump asking him to reverse his executive order and support funding for humanitarian assistance.

And finally, I am extremely troubled by the administration's seeming lack of understanding of the constitutionally-mandated congressional oversight of American military action. If the President intends to escalate our military involvement further, as he has indicated he will consider, then he has a responsibility to send a plan to Congress and seek authorization for any further action. My questions are really—I have two. One is the humanitarian assistance budget is expected to decimated if President Trump's budget is adopted. Would you speak to how these proposed cuts would affect the United States' ability to work toward stability in Syria and in neighboring countries that are taking on the enormous burden of housing the large majority of Syrian refugees, particularly our ally Jordan?

Ms. RAND. Sure. Thank you, Congressman, for that important set of questions.

First on the refugee ban, it is interesting that the media actually hasn't covered the foreign policy disadvantages of the refugee ban because you know Syria's neighbors are taking in four million, five million Syrian refugees. The generosity of the Turks, the Jordanians, the Lebanese, and other neighbors is incredible.

And so you know last year in 2016, the U.S. took in 12,000 Syrian refugees. I mean that is nothing compared to these smaller and less well-off countries. So we are trying to convince our allies surrounding Syria to be generous toward these refugees, to continue to give them housing, to continue to give them education, to continue to work with the U.N. and other international organizations. And that is a really important signal that hasn't been covered. So I just wanted to mention that because we haven't discussed that so far today.

Specifically, on the humanitarian budget, it is unclear because there are still reports of what the cuts will be but the cuts to humanitarian assistance, international development account, the IDA account, cuts to the food aid budget will all significantly affect Syria and its refugees, also the IDPs who have stayed within Syria.

And then the cuts to ESF, to the economic support funds to the Jordanian Government are very concerning. I mean it is just confusing as to why you would cut ESF to one of your closest partners and allies in the region that is both being generous to the Syrian refugees but trying to help you in some of the counterterrorism operations that we have discussed today.

Mr. CICILLINE. Thank you.

Finally, I would just ask any of the panelists, you know we always have discussions about a military solution to this conflict. And I think in the absence of American boots on the ground, which I strongly oppose, I wonder whether there is a military solution and what that would look like. And if not, if it is exclusively a diplomatic solution, what is the strategy or your recommendations as to how we get to that?

Mr. Singh?

Mr. SINGH. Well, thank you, Congressman. I personally say that, as in so many of these situations, there is no exclusively military solution. There is no exclusively diplomatic solution. Ultimately, to the extent our policies are successful, they are successful when we combine all of our tools—diplomatic, military, aid, intelligence, and so forth—and when we do it in conjunction with allies, with a coalition of like-minded countries. And I think that is what is going to be required here.

I do think that, frankly, the April 7th strike is useful in building the credibility of American threats of force. I, for one, would say that it may be that if we already have some American boots on the ground, it may be that there is a role for some more but I don't think it should be the United States in front sort of taking on the heaviest military roles. That should be up to our local partners.

But I think it is going to be force backed by diplomacy, diplomacy backed by force, which is going to be part of the answer here.

Mr. CICILLINE. Anyone else?

Mr. LISTER. I agree.

Mr. CICILLINE. Great. Thank you.

I yield back, Mr. Chairman.

Mr. KINZINGER. The gentleman yields back. The Chair recognizes the gentlelady from Missouri, Ms. Wagner, for 5 minutes.

Ms. WAGNER. Thank you, Mr. Chairman. This is an important hearing. It is high time that the United States grapple strategically with how to end the Syrian conflict.

It is patently clear that there can be no resolution with Assad in power, especially as he continues to prioritize a war against moderate groups seeking democracy over a war against ISIS. His slaughter of innocent civilians is barbaric and the United States cannot hope to defeat ISIS with Assad as the only alternative.

Dr. Rand, the Southern Front has been effective in keeping extremist groups from expanding control in southern Syria. How can we, along with our allies in Israel and Jordan, further support the Southern Front and help them protect against Assad?

Ms. RAND. Thanks, Congresswoman. This is an important issue. And actually because of the focus on Idlib and Aleppo in the past year or so, I think a lot of the attention has shifted away from the Southern Front. So I think it is important to raise it again.

You know a year and a half ago the governance of the Southern Front provided kind of a model of the multiethnic, multisectarian type of governance. They issued a communique talking about inclusion and representations among the different sects. It seemed quite hopeful and seemed potentially a paradigm that could be transported for other parts of Syria.

So the key here I think is two-fold. One is to support the continued moderation of the leadership of the Southern Front to make sure they continue to support different ethnic groups and you know there is some inclusion of al-Qaeda elements, I will let my colleague talk about it, but overall, they have been more moderate than some of the other oppositionists. But second, is just to support them in their counterterrorism needs against ISIS and other more extremists that might challenge their hegemony in this part of Syria.

Ms. WAGNER. Thank you, Dr. Rand.

Mr. Lister, can you discuss coordination between Kurdish forces, such as the SDF, and YPG, and, frankly, and other moderate forces, and I will say local groups? In what ways could the U.S. help advance cooperation between the Kurdish and moderate forces across the country to ensure that areas freed from the Assad regime can, in fact, remain free of terrorism?

Mr. LISTER. Again, that is a very important question. I mean I think what I have tried to focus on in my remarks is to suggest that Syria can't be looked at as a whole. So what we have seen develop in the northeast with the Kurdish YPG and its various allies is one specific component of a much broader reality. What works in the northeast doesn't work in the south. We are not going to see a reflection of the Kurdish Confederation in the northeast suddenly appearing in southern Syria, with a predominately Sunni Arab population.

So I think we should kind of take care of what we have helped to develop in the northeast but we also need to also be aware of the negative knock-on effects of some of these other actors' actions. And so I genuinely am concerned that if we pursue what I think we will pursue, which is a YPG-SDF led offensive on Raqqa, they will very seriously consider whether it takes 1 month or 12 months, some kind of power sharing agreement with the Assad regime.

Ms. WAGNER. Power sharing.

Mr. LISTER. Now that kind—it has already happened. As I said in my opening remarks, in northern Aleppo they have handed territory over to the Assad regime. Now, if that happens in Raqqa, that is a jihadist's dream. It fulfills everything they have said for 6 years, that not only will the West not help protect your civilians but, eventually, they will come in and do their selfish thing, which is fight terrorism and then, eventually, they will give it over to the dictator again. So, we must be very, very careful of preventing a scenario like that from coming true.

And comments from senior military officials here that we have no control over the decisions of our local partners, frankly, is a cop-out.

Ms. WAGNER. It is a cop-out. Thank you for your testimony.

Mr. Singh, the Assad regime uses aerial bombardment and terrorizing weapons to strategically displace the civilian populations in opposition areas. In what ways have Sunni extremist forces and pro-Iranian militias taken advantage of Assad's attacks and displacement of civilians?

Mr. SINGH. Well, I think that is an important question, Congresswoman. And Mr. Lister referred to this before but I think there is no doubt that the brutalization of civilians, the brutalization of the populations is a boon to the extremist groups who, as Mr. Lister pointed out, play on this sort of anti-Assad narrative to boost their own fortunes. And we have seen exactly that occur because we have seen, I think, especially in western Syria, the extremist forces amongst the opposition gain in strength in recent months.

As for the Iranians, the Iranians, I think, are complicit in Assad's actions. And so it is not necessarily right to talk about them gaining from them, they are actually part of those actions because it is the Iranians that I think have the greatest force on the ground backing Assad and I think we need to ascribe blame to them for much of what he does.

Ms. WAGNER. All right, thank you very much. Mr. Chairman, my time has run out.

Mr. GARRETT [presiding]. Thank you. The Chair would now recognize Mr. Suozzi from New York for 5 minutes.

Mr. SUOZZI. Thank you, Mr. Chairman. Let me start by stating the obvious, which is this is incredibly complicated. And I want to thank all of you for sharing your knowledge with us today.

I am going to echo what all of my colleagues have said is that we really need to hear from the administration as to what their plan is to address this very complicated part of the world.

There is an epic struggle going on in the world and, unlike the Cold War, where it was clear that it was the Soviets versus the Americans, this is much more complicated. It is stability versus instability. It is control versus chaos, as Tom Friedman said in his book. And we have gone from 35 million refugees in the world 10 years ago to 65 million refugees today and many of them are from Syria. And as the doctor pointed out in her testimony a few minutes ago, this is destabilizing other countries, as they try and deal with all these refugees in Jordan, and Lebanon, and other countries, in Turkey. And this region is so complicated by the fact there are so many parties involved with Assad—Iran and Russia—and then the rebel forces, America, ISIS, and al-Qaeda, the Turks don't like the Kurds. I mean there are so many pieces here and it is so complicated. But we have to choose in this world that is facing the struggle of stability versus instability where we are going to focus our resources and where we are going to—we have to make choices as to where we are going to pay attention and what we are going to do.

And we have heard from I think it was Brad Sherman before and Congressman Kinzinger about some of these choices we have to make. And for me, you know let's put chemical weapons aside, which I think was a bipartisan, international agreement that we have to combat the best way that we can. But if the choice is between, for right now, what is right in front of us, you have to choose between fighting al-Qaeda and ISIS in Syria, or trying to protect the Syrian people and undoing Assad and forcing to the negotiating table, you have to choose between those two, what is the most important thing in front of the United States right now in our national interest? Is it to combat al-Qaeda and ISIS or is to stop Assad and force him to the negotiating table?

Which is the most important thing before us right now? And you have to choose, each one of you. Mr. Singh, you go first.

Mr. SINGH. Congressman, I am going to disappoint because I think it is a false choice, frankly. I think if you go back to my initial statement, I think in fact we have now sort of several discrete conflicts which are going on within Syria that implicate our interests in the region and implicate the security of our allies. And we can't neglect one for the sake of the other. We have to address all of them.

But it is a mistake to think, as Mr. Lister has said, that we can address all of them together in one neat package, sort of look at them as one problem to be solved. We have to address them in a distinct way.

So in eastern Syria, there is no doubt that our priority has to be al-Qaeda and ISIS.

Mr. SUOZZI. Al-Qaeda and ISIS.

Mr. SINGH. And then not just defeating ISIS but thinking about what comes next because we don't want ISIS to return. But if——

Mr. SUOZZI. Well the focus now is on Raqqa.

Mr. SINGH. On Raqqa, right.

In western Syria, though, absolutely, the continued brutality of the Assad regime, the expansion of Iranian power, the expansion of Hezbollah's power is a tremendous concern not just for us but for Israel, for Turkey, for our allies in the region.

Mr. SUOZZI. Now, I have learned somewhere that 85 percent of the population of Syria is in western Syria. Is that correct?

Mr. SINGH. Correct.

Mr. SUOZZI. Okay.

Mr. SINGH. That is correct.

Mr. LISTER. If I may, briefly. I mentioned in an earlier answer that we have found ourselves capable for about 2 years to combat ISIS primarily in isolation from the rest of the conflict. But we are now discovering that when we reach Raqqa, which is an Arab town, there are big knock-on effects of doing that with certain actors and we are finding, suddenly, the proliferation of knock-on effects along the northern Syrian border.

And it is for that reason that I would agree with my colleague, Mr. Singh, that combating terrorism in Syria and protecting civilians are inextricably linked. Terrorist narratives, no matter what kind of terrorist you are, is linked to the fact that there is suffering, chaos, instability, and brutality in their world.

Mr. SUOZZI. So that is empowering them.

Mr. LISTER. And it is empowering them like nothing else that would be possible. And so I would suggest it is impossible for us to win against terrorism, whatever that might mean, without encompassing in that strategy, the protection of civilians, a de-intensification of the conflict, and challenging the Assad regime's freedom to use any means at his disposal to continue to kill people en masse.

Mr. SUOZZI. Doctor?

Ms. RAND. Thank you. I would agree completely about an inextricability between these two options. And I would give as an example something that we have talked about extensively today that I think exemplifies this.

After Raqqa is liberated, there will be a number of political governance and humanitarian questions before us, essentially, as those who have trained the militias that oust the ISIS terrorists and those include who will govern, whether they are Kurdish or Arab, and how much leverage we can push on them to not hand over to the regime. Those questions will affect how much we can protect the civilians in that liberated area of Syria. And those are things within our purview, within our power, within our leverage through our training and assisting of the partners that will do the liberation.

Mr. SUOZZI. I know my time has expired. I just want to make this one last point.

By us going after ISIS and al-Qaeda, which is in our own self-interest, obviously, and national security, and so we must do it, we are aiding Assad, and Russia, and Iran in the process because they have the same enemy.

Anyway, I am sorry.

Mr. GARRETT. Thank you. The gentleman's time has expired.

The Chair will yield to chair.

I want to be really clear in expressing my high esteem and regard for my honorable colleagues who have spoken earlier, but I have rarely seen such a mind-numbing display of misinformation and disinformation. So, I want to clear some things up.

My colleague from Nevada previously mentioned over 500,000 killed "by the Assad regime." In fact, the Syrian Observatory for Human Rights estimates, and that is the highest estimate of deaths in the conflict, that there have been roughly 500,000 casualties, that about a third of those have been to pro-regime forces, that is deaths.

I presume, then, that Mr. Assad is not responsible for all 500,000 casualties. Is that an accurate assessment, Ms. Rand—Dr. Rand?

Ms. RAND. The different human rights organizations have different estimates. They range between——

Mr. GARRETT. The question is, is President Assad responsible for all half a million deaths in Syria?

Ms. RAND. At least 80 percent of those 500,000.

Mr. GARRETT. Okay, so a fact that a third of the deaths have been to pro-regime forces, you are intimating then that he killed about one-third of that third himself?

Ms. RAND. No, there is also Russian—there are civilians that have not survived because of Russians.

Mr. GARRETT. Right, I would direct your attention to the Syrian Observatory for Human Rights and their statistics.

My colleague from Nevada also made reference to a MOAB drop. That was actually about 2,300 miles away in Afghanistan, right? That wasn't actually in Syria, was it? Yes, so that would be some misinformation.

And then she made reference to no cohesive foreign policy strategy that we have seen from this administration. Mr. Singh, the Trump administration was sworn in about January 20th of 2017. Is that correct?

Mr. SINGH. That is correct.

Mr. GARRETT. Right and so the Syrian civil war really began in earnest, as did other events in the Arab Spring, roughly 2010-2011 and was sort of coopted by first al-Qaeda, and then ISIS moved in to fill a vacuum in the east of the nation, probably about 6 or 7 years ago?

Mr. SINGH. Absolutely right.

Mr. GARRETT. And would you characterize the U.S. foreign policy, particularly through the State Department, from 2011 forward as cohesive and clearly articulated?

Mr. SINGH. Absolutely not; we had no Syria strategy, I think.

Mr. GARRETT. And so if, in fact, U.S. policy is not cohesive and clearly articulated now, that is no departure from the previous 6-plus years?

Mr. SINGH. Well, it certainly isn't but I agree with you, Congressman, that it is still early going. And so my hope is that the Trump administration will be coming forward with a strategy.

Mr. GARRETT. And so too do I. I really do because I would agree that there is not a clearly articulated policy but that there hasn't been one that the previous administration had, by my rough mathematical estimates, about 24 times as much time to formulate one.

So, we also have recent open source intelligence that relates to what has been our stated goal that is to attack and crush ISIS in Syria. And would it not be your agreement, Mr. Lister, that the number of air strikes and attacks directly on ISIS assets since January 20, 2107 have been stepped up and that the apparent success of those attacks is greater than heretofore?

Mr. LISTER. I can't speak personally to have seen statistics that suggest that but it wouldn't surprise me because we are entering, of course, the phase of an intensive operation for Raqqa.

Mr. GARRETT. Okay and there was also an intimation by one of my colleagues that it was inappropriate to have warned the Russians of an impending United States military strike on a facility where Russian forces were probably co-located.

Would you agree with the idea that we shouldn't have let the Russians there were inbound explosive cruise missiles?

Mr. SINGH. Well, I would disagree that it was wrong to do that. I mean we do have deconfliction protocols and, to me, it was prudent to have warned the Russians in the way that we did.

Mr. GARRETT. Right. In fact, had we not warned the Russians, the Russians might have been even more incensed by the American action without any sort of heads up, if you will pardon the colloquialism.

Now, were there regime chemical weapons attacks prior to the assumption of power of the Trump administration?

Mr. SINGH. Yes, there sure were.

Mr. GARRETT. Okay. And there were also chemical weapons attacks, to be fair, perpetrated by Jabhat al-Nusra/Jabhat Fateh al-Sham, obviously a renaming of al-Nusra, who was sort of infiltrated by al-Qaeda. They have used chlorine as well, we think, as has ISIS.

Mr. SINGH. So I am not sure I have the best information but I think I would draw a distinction between the types of chemical attacks, sarin attacks, and so forth, and the types of attacks you are talking about, Congressman.

Mr. GARRETT. Okay. Is it fair to say that there aren't a whole lot of clean hands as it goes around to atrocities committed in Syria? For example, you know setting aflame a Jordanian captured pilot wasn't perpetrated, to our knowledge, by the regime.

Mr. SINGH. There have been atrocities committed by several sides in this conflict.

Mr. GARRETT. Sure. In fact, I would argue everybody.

Ms. RAND. Congressman, I would just add on that point there is no moral equivalency between the regime has done and what the other actors have done. I mean the regime is responsible for the vast amount of the destruction.

Mr. GARRETT. Okay. Well, I haven't asked this question yet but so let me make sure I understand this right.

Okay, we have ISIS. We understand who they are. We have got Jabhat Fateh al-Sham, who is sort of a derivative of al-Nusra. It is fair to say that al-Nusra was sort of coopted by al-Qaeda. Correct?

In the north, regionally strong we have YPG and Kurds but they don't have any real desire, based on tribal affinity, to rule the nation, or the nation accept a Kurdish-led rule.

And so if we are going to start establishing moral equivalencies, then would we rather ISIS, al-Qaeda, or the Assad regime to be in charge? Now, that is a rhetorical question.

The bottom line I think that I am driving at is, before we engage in regime change activities, we ought to have a plan on who is going to fill the vacuum that we create because what five and a half million to six and a half million displaced people have in common is they didn't want to be displaced. But this nation led from behind, in our own words, and worked to create vacuums by encouraging uprising and revolts without any regard for who would fill the vacuum. And we saw Christians beheaded on the beaches in Libya, and we see half a million dead by the hands of many bloody actors in Syria, and we are partly responsible.

We should not engage in regime change activities without contemplating who fills the vacuum that we create. Would you agree, Mr. Lister?

Mr. LISTER. Frankly speaking, it is not about regime change. It is about upholding international norms to ensure that governments don't commit repeated war crimes on a daily basis. And our objective, so far as I am concerned, is not regime change, we are not invading the country like we did in Iraq, it is to set up conditions that will allow a political process to be more meaningful and for all actors on all sides to treat it seriously.

Mr. GARRETT. So I couldn't agree more. And that sort of jives with what Secretary Tillerson had indicated to the Russians before the missile strike on the airfield. That is, we don't have to see Assad go but we have to see stability and peace in the region. That should be our goal.

Mr. LISTER. Well, I mean, the conclusion of the political process is up to Syrians. I think we ought to have, morally, a conclusion that Assad should go but it is not our choice to make that decision. But it is our responsibility, as a significant portion of the international community, to allow all Syrians to have that choice.

Mr. GARRETT. Right.

Mr. LISTER. And they haven't had it for 6 years.

Mr. GARRETT. Right, absolutely. Thank you. And I have gone way over.

Mr. ENGEL. Will the gentleman yield?

Mr. GARRETT. I have gone way over so I would not yield.

Mr. ENGEL. You would not yield?

Mr. GARRETT. I am out of time.

Mr. ENGEL. You could still yield to me. You are in the chair.

Mr. GARRETT. I am not going to yield.

Mr. ENGEL. You are not going to yield? Well, I am sorry that the bipartisanship that we have had here for so many years, that you don't follow the lead of the chairman and myself.

Mr. GARRETT. Well, I apologize.

Mr. ENGEL. I am really very sorry about that.

Mr. GARRETT. I forgive you.

Mr. ENGEL. I have been on this committee——

Mr. GARRETT. I——

Mr. ENGEL. I don't need your forgiveness.

Mr. GARRETT. I don't understand the——

Mr. ENGEL. I don't need your forgiveness.

Mr. GARRETT. Well, you have been on this committee long enough to know the protocol and I don't.

Mr. ENGEL. Long enough to know——

Mr. GARRETT. So, I will yield you 30 seconds.

Mr. ENGEL. Thank you. It is common courtesy that people are yielded time when they ask their colleagues.

Let me just say, first of all, that when I grew up I learned from my parents that two wrongs don't make a right. Many of us on this side of the aisle were critical of the previous administration and what it did, and we said so at the time. There is no reason to not be critical of what is happening with the current administration just because the administration didn't do what should have been done.

I will agree with you, and I have been saying this for years, that we made a misstep when we did not aid and abet, help the Free Syrian Army way back when. And we made a mistake when the previous President drew a line in the sand and then didn't follow through.

But that doesn't absolve the current administration from its responsibility. And its responsibility has been that it needs to come to Congress with any plan that it has. It needs to tell us what their attempts are in Syria and what their goals are.

We have learned for many, many years, giving any administration a blank check to create war is not something that this Congress should do.

And I think there is no doubt in my mind, and in everybody else's mind, that Assad is really the butcher of Syria. That yes, there have been killings on both sides, but it was the Assad regime's reaction to the Arab Spring when peaceful Syrians went out to demonstrate against their dictatorial government that Assad decided he would respond with deadly force.

And so I blame all the atrocities that happened in Syria on the bloody hands of Assad because had he not acted the way he acted, this would not have happened.

I just want to set the record straight. I do agree that there were missteps by the previous administration but that doesn't mean that we have to overlook missteps by this administration.

I yield back.

Mr. GARRETT. Thank you and I apologize again to Mr. Engel, as it relates to not yielding. I did not, literally, know the protocol of the committee. So I will take that lump.

I want to thank the time of the witnesses today. These are very critical issues. Your expertise and insight is important and I think, candidly, despite the tone that some of this took, we all want the same thing, and that is a world in which people can live where they choose to live, free from fear of persecution or death. And Syria is one where, if we ultimately get it right, we might take a good step in the right direction toward ensuring that going forward in the future because it is certainly a tough rubric.

Thank you very much.

[Whereupon, at 12:47 p.m., the committee was adjourned.]

A P P E N D I X

MATERIAL SUBMITTED FOR THE RECORD

FULL COMMITTEE HEARING NOTICE
COMMITTEE ON FOREIGN AFFAIRS
U.S. HOUSE OF REPRESENTATIVES
WASHINGTON, DC 20515-6128

Edward R. Royce (R-CA), Chairman

April 27, 2017

TO: MEMBERS OF THE COMMITTEE ON FOREIGN AFFAIRS

You are respectfully requested to attend an OPEN hearing of the Committee on Foreign Affairs, to be held in Room 2172 of the Rayburn House Office Building (and available live on the Committee website at http://www.ForeignAffairs.house.gov):

DATE: Thursday, April 27, 2017

TIME: 10:00 a.m.

SUBJECT: Syria After the Missile Strikes: Policy Options

WITNESSES: Mr. Michael Singh
                   Lane-Swig Senior Fellow
                   Managing Director
                   The Washington Institute for Near East Policy

                   Mr. Charles Lister
                   Senior Fellow
                   Middle East Institute

                   Dafna H. Rand, Ph.D.
                   Adjunct Professor
                   National Defense University

By Direction of the Chairman

COMMITTEE ON FOREIGN AFFAIRS
MINUTES OF FULL COMMITTEE HEARING

Day __*Thursday*__ Date __*4/27/2017*__ Room __*2172*__

Starting Time __*10:07*__ Ending Time __*12:47*__

Recesses __*0*__ (___ to ___)(___ to ___)(___ to ___)(___ to ___)(___ to ___)(___ to ___)

Presiding Member(s)
Chairman Edward R. Royce

Check all of the following that apply:

Open Session ✓
Executive (closed) Session ☐
Televised ✓

Electronically Recorded (taped) ✓
Stenographic Record ✓

TITLE OF HEARING:

Syria After the Missile Strikes: Policy Options

COMMITTEE MEMBERS PRESENT:

See attached.

NON-COMMITTEE MEMBERS PRESENT:

none

HEARING WITNESSES: Same as meeting notice attached? Yes ✓ No ☐
(If "no", please list below and include title, agency, department, or organization.)

STATEMENTS FOR THE RECORD: *(List any statements submitted for the record.)*

IFR - Rep. Eliot Engel
SFR - Rep. Gerald Connolly

TIME SCHEDULED TO RECONVENE _____
or
TIME ADJOURNED __*12:47*__

_____
Full Committee Hearing Coordinator

80

HOUSE COMMITTEE ON FOREIGN AFFAIRS
FULL COMMITTEE HEARING

PRESENT	MEMBER	PRESENT	MEMBER
X	Edward R. Royce, CA	X	Eliot L. Engel, NY
	Christopher H. Smith, NJ	X	Brad Sherman, CA
X	Ileana Ros-Lehtinen, FL	X	Gregory W. Meeks, NY
X	Dana Rohrabacher, CA	X	Albio Sires, NJ
	Steve Chabot, OH	X	Gerald E. Connolly, VA
X	Joe Wilson, SC	X	Theodore E. Deutch, FL
X	Michael T. McCaul, TX		Karen Bass, CA
X	Ted Poe, TX	X	William Keating, MA
	Darrell Issa, CA	X	David Cicilline, RI
	Tom Marino, PA	X	Ami Bera, CA
X	Jeff Duncan, SC	X	Lois Frankel, FL
X	Mo Brooks, AL	X	Tulsi Gabbard, HI
	Paul Cook, CA		Joaquin Castro, TX
X	Scott Perry, PA	X	Robin Kelly, IL
	Ron DeSantis, FL	X	Brendan Boyle, PA
	Mark Meadows, NC	X	Dina Titus, NV
X	Ted Yoho, FL	X	Norma Torres, CA
X	Adam Kinzinger, IL	X	Brad Schneider, IL
X	Lee Zeldin, NY	X	Tom Suozzi, NY
	Dan Donovan, NY	X	Adriano Espaillat, NY
	James F. Sensenbrenner, Jr., WI	X	Ted Lieu, CA
X	Ann Wagner, MO		
X	Brian J. Mast, FL		
X	Brian K. Fitzpatrick, PA		
	Francis Rooney, FL		
X	Thomas A. Garrett, Jr., VA		

MATERIAL SUBMITTED FOR THE RECORD BY THE HONORABLE ELIOT L. ENGEL, A REPRESENTATIVE IN CONGRESS FROM THE STATE OF NEW YORK

A statement by Raed al-Saleh, head of the Syria Civil Defense also known as the White Helmets, on behalf of the Nobel Peace Prize nominated rescue organization that has rescued over 90,000 Syrian lives:

"After President Obama failed to uphold his "red line" and let Assad put Syria into a six year spiral of horror and destruction, Syrians have found hope in President Trump's resolve to reassert the international community's intolerance towards the use of chemical weapons.

We now wait to see if the United States will lead an international effort to help protect Syrians from other brutal regime tactics, and to help ensure a political solution is achieved, which brings peace to our country, holds war criminals accountable, and ensures Syrians have full control over their political future without interference by any outside powers.

As humanitarian rescue workers who hold no affiliation to any political or religious faction or group, we only want to see an immediate end to the violence so that we can get on and rebuild our beloved country. We believe it is within the powers of the international community to put an end to the aerial bombardment, and to breathe new life into the political negotiations that must bring an end to the war."

MATERIAL SUBMITTED FOR THE RECORD BY THE HONORABLE ELIOT L. ENGEL, A
REPRESENTATIVE IN CONGRESS FROM THE STATE OF NEW YORK

CWS Statement to the U.S. House Foreign Affairs Committee, pertaining to its hearing
Syria After the Missile Strikes: Policy Options
Thursday, April 27, 2017

As a 71-year old humanitarian organization representing 37 Protestant, Anglican, and Orthodox communions and 34 refugee resettlement offices across the country, Church World Service (CWS) calls on the U.S. government to extend welcome to Syrian refugees, strengthen its support for a humanitarian protection response, and urge the international community to do the same. We cannot sit idly by while our Syrian brothers and sisters seek safety from violence that has forced them from their homes. We should carry on our nation's proud history of hospitality and leadership.

More than eight million Syrians are internally displaced and 4.8 million Syrian refugees are seeking safety in the region,[1] especially in host countries like Lebanon, Jordan, Turkey, Iraq, and Egypt. The combination of deteriorating conditions in refugee hosting countries and the lack of safe, legal, and timely access to protection forces men, women, and children to take perilous journeys and risk falling prey to traffickers, exploitation, or losing their lives. As the recent chemical attacks and heartbreaking deaths of innocent children and adults in Syria demonstrate, Syrian families are in desperate need of humanitarian assistance. These horrors and the subsequent U.S. military action in Syria highlight the dire need and responsibility we have to protect refugees fleeing these realities. This includes offering vulnerable individuals safety through resettlement.

The humanitarian crisis in Syria is complex, requiring U.S. and international leadership on comprehensive solutions. Chemical weapons, barrel bombs, indiscriminate shelling, and the terror of ISIS are what Syrian refugees have been escaping for the last six years. As the conflict in Syria now enters a new phase with increased U.S. involvement, it is critical the U.S. government expands our nation's refugee resettlement program. We can – and must – admit more refugees fleeing these terrors. Resettlement aligns with our foreign policy goals and plays a strategic diplomatic role in alleviating pressure on host countries in the region and galvanizing international action. The U.S. refugee resettlement program is a lifesaving, public-private partnership that provides refugees an opportunity to rebuild their lives in safety. U.S. communities, schools, congregations, and employers welcome refugees and help them integrate in their new homes. In turn, refugees contribute to their new communities with their innovative skills, dedicated work, and inspiring perseverance.

Durable solutions require sufficient resources and timely protection to help refugees integrate and rebuild their lives. The United States must continue its support to UNHCR, humanitarian organizations, and refugee hosting countries to ensure infrastructure can adequately support refugees. It is imperative that wherever they are, refugees have the freedom to move, the right to work, and the ability for their children to attend school. All countries' migration and refugee policies should be rooted in a humanitarian, rights-based, and hospitable approach. Every effort must be made to save the lives of refugees and migrants in jeopardy, including expanding protection space and increasing the capacity of civilian search and rescue operations for migrants in transit, including at sea. We urge governments to expand legal and safe avenues for people to seek safety, to expedite procedures so that people have timely access to protection, and to enhance family tracing and reunification capacities.

People of faith across the globe have already demonstrated the best of humanity through acts of welcome through the U.S. refugee resettlement program, the importance of which should be affirmed by the U.S. government. The hospitality, welcome, and cooperation of communities are powerful antidotes to dangerous xenophobic, discriminatory rhetoric and anti-Muslim sentiments. All vulnerable persons in need of protection must be welcomed, regardless of their faith or ethnicity. We encourage Members of Congress to maintain regular dialogue and collaboration with civil society, including congregations and faith-based organizations, as they are eager to help refugees with both immediate needs and longer-term integration assistance. Thousands of Syrian refugees are already at various stages of the rigorous U.S. resettlement screening process, including many who have already been approved by the Department of Homeland Security. Despite the U.S. government putting in place mechanisms to allow Syrian refugees to reunite with their family members who are already U.S. citizens and Lawful Permanent Residents[2], many such cases are still pending and require immediate attention. The United States can and must do more to resettle Syrian refugees.

CWS urges the United States to work with the international community to provide a comprehensive response to the humanitarian crisis in Syria by strengthening access to protection and welcoming refugees impacted by the Syrian conflict. CWS stands committed to working with both chambers of Congress and the Administration to resettle Syrian refugees as part of our foreign policy interests and humanitarian responsibilities. We urge all Members of Congress to demonstrate the best of American heart and hospitality by agreeing to resettle more refugees this year and into the future.

---

[1] United Nations High Commissioner for Refugees, UNHCR: 1 in 10 Syrian refugees will need resettling, Mar. 29, 2016, http://www.unhcr.org/56fa71f39.html. For more statistics, see United Nations Office of Humanitarian Affairs, Syrian Arab Republic, http://www.unocha.org/syria/.
[2] "U.S. Refugee Resettlement Processing for Iraqi and Syrian Beneficiaries of an Approved I-130 Petition." Bureau of Population, Refugees and Migration. <www.state.gov/j/prm/releases/factsheets/2016/254349.htm>.

Statement for the Record
Submitted by Mr. Connolly of Virginia

On April 4, 2017, the Syrian government of President Bashar al-Assad carried out an unspeakable attack on the northern Syria town of Khan Sheikhoun. The horrendous sarin gas attack killed roughly 100 people, including scores of children. Unfortunately, this Committee can no longer be shocked by the extent of Assad's brutality.

The Assad regime has perpetrated atrocities on the Syrian civilian population -- including sectarian violence, mass killings, torture, and the use of chemical weapons and barrel bombs – and it shows no signs of subsiding. Just days before the most recent chemical attack, U.S. Ambassador to the United Nations Nikki Haley stated that it was no longer a priority of the United States to remove Assad from power, effectively telling Assad that he could continue such murderous treatment of his own people.

On April 6, 2017, the United States conducted airstrikes targeting Syrian war planes and infrastructure at al-Shayrat airfield in Homs Province. The United States and the international community must respond to the use of chemical weapons. However, fifty-nine Tomahawk cruise missiles are not a substitute for a strategy going forward. A kneejerk kinetic response without an overarching military strategy endangers American lives and diminishes U.S. global leadership. The Trump Administration must begin a dialogue with Congress about our Syria policy.

We should be clear-eyed about the conditions under which these events have taken place. The Syrian civil war has raged for more than six years. Conflict between government forces, terrorist organizations, and opposition groups has engulfed the country. Operations to support competing factions of the civil war have pitted the interests of world powers against one another and forced all sides to wrestle with the specter of an expanded conflict. There are 13.5 million Syrians in need of humanitarian assistance inside Syria, and nearly 5 million Syrians have registered as refugees in neighboring countries and beyond. This crush of humanity has strained resources within those countries, drastically changed regional demographics, and destabilized neighboring countries.

Amidst this backdrop, the United States has a variety of interests at stake in Syria, including counterterrorism efforts and the fight against ISIL, alleviating humanitarian concerns, enforcing global norms against chemical weapons, and broader regional stability. Congress and the Administration must embark on an effort to define for our allies, our constituents, and the Syrian people how we will protect these interests.

If President Trump intends to engage in further military action, then the War Powers Resolution requires that he obtain authorization from Congress within 60 days. The clock started with Trump's airstrikes on April 6. U.S. sanctions have not effectively cut off the flow of money and supplies to the Assad regime. The Caesar Syria Civilian Protection Act (H.R. 1677), of which I am a cosponsor, would impose new sanctions on Syrian human rights abusers and those who facilitate the Assad regime's atrocities. I am pleased that this Committee will be marking up this bill next week. H.R. 1677 also encourages negotiations to bring about a lasting political solution. A negotiated settlement is the only way to end this conflict, but the Trump Administration has decimated U.S. diplomatic capabilities by failing to fill senior State Department positions and proposing draconian cuts to U.S. development and diplomacy programs.

This crisis cannot end while a civil war rages on. Ultimately, it is political negotiations that will bring lasting relief to the millions of affected Syrians who have known only violence and displacement for more than six years. I look forward to hearing from our witnesses regarding how the United States can navigate the protracted chaos of the Syrian saga and articulate a strategy to protect its interests in Syria.

www.ingramcontent.com/pod-product-compliance
Lightning Source LLC
Chambersburg PA
CBHW081230280526
45787CB00006B/2592